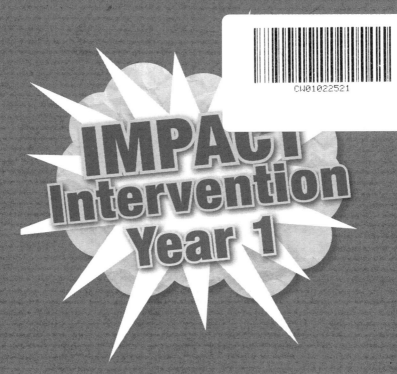

IMPACT Intervention Year 1

Stephen Monaghan and Melissa Blackwood

Published by Keen Kite Books
An imprint of HarperCollins*Publishers* Ltd
The News Building
1 London Bridge Street
London
SE1 9GF

Text and design © 2017 Keen Kite Books, an imprint of HarperCollins*Publishers* Ltd

10 9 8 7 6 5 4 3 2 1

ISBN 978-0-00-822838-5

The author asserts their moral right to be identified as the author of this work.

British Library Cataloguing in Publication Data

A catalogue record for this publication is available from the British Library.

Authors: Stephen Monaghan and Melissa Blackwood
Contributor: Charlotte Monaghan
Commissioning Editors: Shelley Teasdale and Michelle l'Anson
Project Manager: Fiona Watson
Editor: Denise Moulton
Internal design and illustrations: QBS Learning
Production: Lyndsey Rogers

Introduction

Impact Intervention is a new series of resources created by teachers and aimed at teaching assistants, classroom assistants, NQTs and time-strapped teachers.

The books include tried and tested ready-to-go activities that are intended for use with small groups of pupils to help scaffold learning.

The resources can be used to deliver pre-teach sessions, booster interventions or breakout sessions after lessons to pick up pupils who are struggling to achieve a learning outcome.

Impact Intervention can be dipped into as needed and used with minimal preparation.

The books contain:
- standalone sessions with activities that focus on an achievable part of a learning objective
- content that has been broken down into small steps so that it is easy to follow and deliver
- activities that can be easily implemented in a 15–20-minute session without the need to read through lots of information in advance
- probing questions, prompts and key checks to help assess pupils' knowledge and understanding
- support and extension ideas.

Each title in the series contains content that is robust, age-appropriate and adheres to the standard of the KS1 / KS2 English and maths programmes of study.

Contents

IMPACT Intervention

Maths Activities

Human counting

Strand: Number – number and place value

Learning objective: To count amounts of objects in ones, twos, fives and tens.

You will need: whiteboards, whiteboard pens, number lines

1. **Say:** *Today we will be using our bodies to count.* **Ask:** *What could we use to count in twos?* The pupils might suggest eyes, ears, hands or feet, but try to steer them towards eyes or ears. (Explain that feet and hands will be used later.)

2. **Ask:** *How many pairs of eyes do we have in this room?* Count in twos to find out how many eyes there are.

3. **Ask:** *Can you draw this on your whiteboard?* The pupils should draw pairs of eyes and number them in twos and write the total, e.g.

4. Repeat the task counting in fives using fingers.

5. Repeat the task counting in tens using toes.

Key checks: Can the pupils count eyes in twos, hands in fives and pairs of feet in tens? Are the pupils using the key vocabulary: twos, fives, tens, zero, one to twenty (and beyond), digit, number?

Extension: Challenge the pupils to find out how many eyes, fingers and thumbs or toes there are in the whole class.

Support: Provide the pupils with a number line to help them count in twos, fives or tens if needed.

Penny pincher

Strand: Number – number and place value

Learning objective: To count amounts of objects in ones, twos, fives and tens (including counting 1ps, 2ps, 5ps, 10ps).

You will need: plastic or real 1p, 2p, 5p and 10p coins, number lines or 100 squares

1. **Say:** *Today you will be using money to count in ones, twos, fives and tens.*

2. **Ask:** *Who goes shopping with an adult? What do people use to pay for their shopping?* (The pupils might say card, phone, smart watch or money/cash.)

3. Show the pupils the money and discuss which are the 1p, 2p, 5p and 10p coins.

4. **Ask:** *Can you count to 10 using the 1p coins?* Do this as a group.

5. **Ask:** *Can you count to 20 using the 2p coins?* Do this as a group.

6. Repeat for counting to 50 in 5p coins and to 100 in 10p coins.

7. Repeat for counting to 50 using 5p and then 2p coins.

8. Repeat for counting to 100 (£1) with 10p and then 5p coins.

9. Write some numbers on the board and ask the pupils to make these numbers using the money they have in front of them (e.g. 15, 27 or 35).

Key checks: Do the pupils understand that there are no 3p, 4p, 6p, 7p, 8p or 9p coins? Are the pupils using the key vocabulary: ones, twos, fives, tens, money, coin, pence, pound, how many, total?

Extension: Challenge the pupils to count to 20 using a mixture of the coins.

Support: Provide a number line or 100 square to help the pupils visualise. Show the pupils how two 1p coins equal one 2p coin, five 1p coins equal one 5p coin, and ten 1p coins equal one 10p coin. Provide them with eight 2p coins and ask them to count in twos to see how much is there. (16p)

One more, one less

Strand: Number – number and place value

Learning objective: To find one more or one less.

You will need: counters, 11 whiteboards, whiteboard pen, number lines, 100 squares, die

1. Show the pupils two counters. **Ask:** *What would happen if we added one more counter?* Make a note of the pupils' responses (e.g. 'There will be more', 'There will be three').

2. Add one more counter. Together **say:** *2 add 1 equals 3.*

3. Together create a number line from 0–10 on the floor using 11 evenly spaced whiteboards with the numbers 0–10 written on them.

4. **Ask:** *What is one more than 3?* Ask a pupil to stand by the 3 on the number line and to jump forwards 1. **Say:** *3 + 1 = 4.*

5. **Ask:** *What is one less than 6?* Ask one pupil to jump back from 6 to 5. Encourage the other pupils to show this on their individual number lines or 100 squares. **Say:** *6 – 1 = 5.*

6. Roll a die. **Ask:** *What is your number?* (e.g. Roll a 5 and say 'My number is 5'.)

7. **Ask:** *Do you know how we could find one more than this number?* Take suggestions. **Say:** *I could count on: 1, 2, 3, 4, 5, 6. One more than 5 is 6.*

8. Repeat the activity for one less using the number line created earlier.

Key checks: Can the pupils demonstrate one more and one less using a number line, a 100 square or hands-on equipment? Are the pupils using the key vocabulary: one more, one less, more than, less than, count on, count back, forwards, backwards?

Extension: Ask the pupils to tell you two more and two less than a number and then progress to 10 more and 10 less.

Support: Use numbers below 10 and encourage the pupils to use a number line or a 100 square to help them explain their thinking.

Perfect position

Strand: Number – number and place value

Learning objective: To order numbers (in position on a number line and 100 square).

You will need: whiteboards, whiteboard pens, 0–10 and 0–20 number cards (or toys labelled 0–10 and 0–20), number lines or 100 squares

1. **Say:** *Today you will be ordering numbers.*

2. Ask the pupils to draw a number line from 0–10 on their whiteboards to check their prior knowledge.

3. On the board, draw a number line from 0–10 with some numbers missing.

4. **Ask:** *What numbers are missing from this number line? How do you know?* (The pupils are likely to link their responses to one more/one less, odd and even numbers and number bonds to 10.)

5. Randomly distribute the 0–10 number cards or toys.

6. **Say:** *Let's work together to put these number cards (toys) in the correct order.*

7. Repeat the activity with numbers 0–20.

Key checks: Can the pupils explain their thoughts about number order using concrete materials or drawings? Are the pupils using the key vocabulary: one more/one less, odd numbers, even numbers, number bonds to 10?

Extension: Provide a 100 square with some numbers missing and ask the pupils to offer mathematical reasoning as to what the missing numbers should be. (e.g. 'I know this number is 31 because it is in the 30s; is one more than 30; is one less than 32; is odd and has a 1 in the ones column.') Focus on numbers below 30 and then progress.

Support: Provide the pupils with a number line or 100 square so they can see the numbers in order as well as a visual representation using containers of toys.

Pencil problems

Strand: Number – number and place value

Learning objective: To identify and represent numbers using objects and pictorial representations.

You will need: a variety of objects (e.g. 1 pencil, 2 cubes, 3 rulers, 4 gluesticks, up to 20), 1–20 number cards, counters, ten frames or building blocks

1. Start with 1–10. Place the objects you have gathered on a table in clear piles.

2. **Ask:** *How many pencils do I have here?* Repeat with the other objects.

3. **Ask:** *Which pile has the smallest number of objects? How do you know? Are there more or less rulers than pencils? How do you know?*

4. Distribute the number cards to the pupils. **Ask:** *Which of these number cards goes with each pile?* The pupils pair up each number card with a pile of objects. **Ask:** *How do you know that you are correct?*

5. Give the pupils some counters. **Ask:** *Can you make the counters match the number card?* Ask the pupils to put the correct amount of counters by each number card. Repeat for numbers of objects from 1–20, focusing on teen numbers.

6. **Ask:** *What do you notice about teen numbers?* (Each number has 1 ten and a number of ones.) *Can you think of a way to represent 10? Can you create your own visual representation to show your thinking for the numbers 10–19? How will your drawing change when you reach 20?*

Key checks: Do the pupils know the difference between 12 and 21 (discuss the position of each number)? Can the pupils explain their thinking using the correct statements? Are the pupils using the key vocabulary: equal to, more than, less than (fewer), most, least?

Extension: Challenge the pupils to say some less than/more than/most/least statements about the objects. Can they make the objects equal to each other? Ask the pupils to create their own object collection showing the numbers 1–20 and offer more than, less than and equal to number stories.

Support: Encourage the pupils to focus on the most and least numbers. Then link this to 'most' being more than the least number and 'least' being less than the most number. They may use a ten frame or build a tower to show these numbers.

Addition number bonds

Strand: Number – addition and subtraction

Learning objective: To know addition bonds to 10 and to 20.

You will need: box of cubes/counters/Numicon/Dienes/multi-base arithmetic blocks, ten frames, number lines or 100 squares, 0–20 number cards

1. **Ask:** *What is addition?* Record the pupils' responses.

2. **Ask:** *What other words are there for addition?* (They may suggest: add, more, plus, make, sum, total, altogether.)

3. Write the numbers 1, 4, 7 and 9 on the board. **Ask:** *How many more do we need to add to each number to make 10?*

4. Use the apparatus to allow the pupils to see/find out how to do this. Each pupil should respond. **Ask:** *Why do you think that? Can you explain why? Can you show your thinking using the equipment?*

5. **Ask:** *Is there a way we can check this?* (The pupils may suggest putting the 10 Numicon on top of their own suggestion; placing the 10 Dienes next to their cubes; using a number line with jumps; drawing or verbally counting them. They may even use a ten frame.) If using Numicon, discuss how an odd number has one 'popping up' and even numbers are 'flat'.

6. Write the numbers 2, 5, 8 and 3 on the board. **Ask:** *Can you say a number sentence to make each number add to 10?* The pupils show you this using the equipment provided.

7. Once the pupils have shown they know number bonds to 10, use the same methods for number bonds to 20.

Key checks: Are the pupils using the appropriate strategies for bonds (e.g. 7 + 3 or 3 + 7)? Are they using the key vocabulary: add, more, plus, make, sum, total, equals, altogether?

Extension: Offer the pupils number cards from 1–20 to arrange into number sentences to make 10 or 20. Ask the pupils to write how to make 14 (10 + 4), 17 (10 + 7), etc.

Support: Allow the pupils to use cubes or their fingers and start by asking them to create number bonds to 5 to build their confidence.

Subtraction number bonds

Strand: Number – addition and subtraction

Learning objective: To know subtraction bonds to 10 and 20.

You will need: 0–9 dice, 10–19 dice (or use 0–20 number cards to generate digits), box of cubes/counters/Numicon/Dienes/multi-base arithmetic blocks, number lines or 100 squares, whiteboards, whiteboard pens

1. Recap number bond addition (e.g. write 6 on the board and **ask:** *What do we have to add to make 10? To make 20?)* Give the pupils time to use the equipment, if needed. Ensure the pupils have an understanding of addition before moving on to subtraction.

2. Write the number 10 on the board. Roll a 0–9 die to generate a number (e.g. 6) and subtract the number from 10. **Say:** *10 – 6 = 4.* Make sure you are using the correct vocabulary.

3. Write the calculation on the board (e.g. 10 – 6 =) and use the cubes to show this calculation.

4. Write 20 on the board and roll either the 0–9 die or the 10–19 die to generate a number (e.g. 12). Subtract the number from 20. **Say:** *20 – 12 = 8.*

5. Write the calculation on the board (e.g. 20 – 12 =) and use the cubes to show this calculation.

6. Allow the pupils to practise this with their own dice. They can try both addition and subtraction calculations, using the equipment for support if needed.

7. **Say:** *Addition and subtraction are the 'inverse' of each other. For example, if we start with 6 and add 4, it equals 10. Then, if we subtract 4 from 10, we get back to 6.*

Key checks: Can the pupils use equipment or drawing to explain their thinking and demonstrate their understanding? Are the pupils using the key vocabulary: less than, subtract, minus, take away, difference between?

Extension: Write missing number sentences for the pupils to solve, using equipment if needed (e.g. ? – 4 = 6, ? – 7 = 3, ? – 7 = 13). **Ask:** *What could the missing number be? Why do you think this?*

Support: Encourage the pupils to use cubes or their fingers and start by asking them to use bonds to 5 to build their confidence.

Addition and subtraction number bonds

Strand: Number – addition and subtraction

Learning objective: To know addition and subtraction bonds to 10 and 20.

You will need: box of cubes/counters/Numicon/Dienes/multi-base arithmetic blocks, number lines or 100 squares, 0–20 number cards, whiteboards, whiteboard pens

1. Recap addition and subtraction number bonds. For example, write 8 on the board and **ask:** *What do we have to add to make 10? To make 20?* Write 14 on the board and **ask:** *What do we have to do to 14 to get the answer 10?* Give the pupils time to use the equipment, if needed.

2. Write the numbers 12, 18 and 16 on the board.

3. **Ask:** *What do we have to do to each number to make 10?* Take each pupil's suggestion. **Ask:** *Why do you think that? Can you explain why? How could you find out?*

4. Show the pupils how to count backwards using a number line. Count back from 12 to 10, clearly stating 1 ... 2 as you count backwards. **Say:** *We need to count back 2 to make 10 from 12.*

5. Write the numbers 19, 17, 14 and 13 on the board. **Ask:** *Can you make a number sentence that turns each number into 10 by subtracting?* The pupils show you this using the equipment provided.

Key checks: Can the pupils use equipment or drawing to explain their thinking and demonstrate their understanding? Are the pupils using the key vocabulary: more, less, add, plus, make, sum, total, equals, altogether, subtract, minus, take away, difference between?

Extension: Give the pupils a variety of number sentences with some digits missing. Begin with addition (e.g. 6 + ? = 10) and move on to subtraction when they are confident (e.g. 15 – ? = 10 or ? – 5 = 10).

Support: Encourage the pupils to use cubes or their fingers and start by asking them to create bonds to 5 to build their confidence.

Addition sentences

Strand: Number – addition and subtraction

Learning objective: To read, write and interpret mathematical statements involving addition (+).

You will need: objects (e.g. cubes or pencils), whiteboards, whiteboard pens, number lines or 100 squares

1. Recap one more and one less with the pupils. Show them four objects (e.g. cubes) and **ask:** *If I added one more cube, how many cubes would I have?* Allow the pupils time to respond.

2. Add a cube. **Ask:** *How many cubes are there now?*

3. Put two more cubes on the table, separate from the first group. **Ask:** *How many cubes are in the new pile?*

4. **Ask:** *How many cubes do we have altogether?* Observe the use of any key language, (e.g. add, altogether, addition). Create a number sentence together (5 + 2 = 7).

5. Now mix up the seven cubes on the table. **Ask:** *Using the cubes on the table, can you make a different addition number sentence?* Tell the pupils to use their whiteboards and some cubes. The pupils record their number sentence on their whiteboards, as a drawing if they prefer, and then bring the cubes together to create a total of 7. They should be able to write the + and = symbols in the correct place (e.g. 2 cubes + 5 cubes = 7 cubes or 4 cubes + 3 cubes = 7 cubes).

6. Discuss the number sentences that have been created, using the correct vocabulary.

7. Repeat this activity with different numbers.

Key checks: Can the pupils explain their thinking by using the objects to show number sentences? Are the pupils using the key vocabulary: more, altogether, total, equals, sum, add, increase?

Extension: Encourage the pupils to make addition number sentences without using cubes. This can be done either verbally or they can be written down.

Support: If pupils are struggling to use the objects, allow them to use their fingers, a 100 square or a number line to add.

Subtraction sentences

Strand: Number – addition and subtraction

Learning objective: To read, write and interpret mathematical statements involving subtraction (–).

You will need: objects (e.g. cubes or pencils), whiteboards, whiteboard pens, number lines

1. Recap addition with the pupils and create a number sentence together using the equipment (e.g. 6 + 4 = 10).

2. **Ask:** *What is the inverse of addition?* (subtraction) **Say:** *For example, if we start with 6 and add 4, it equals 10. Then, if we subtract 4 from 10, we get back to 6.*

3. Place five cubes on the table. **Ask:** *What would happen if we took two cubes away from five cubes?* Observe the use of key language (e.g. take away, subtract, less than and equals). Create a number sentence together: 5 – 2 = 3.

4. Discuss the different symbols: + means add and – means subtract.

5. Mix up the cubes on the table. **Ask:** *Using the cubes on the table, can you make a different subtraction number sentence?* Tell the pupils to use their whiteboards and some cubes. The pupils record their number sentence on their whiteboard, as a drawing if they prefer, and then remove cubes to show the answer to the calculation. They should be able to write the – and = symbols in the correct place (e.g. 5 cubes – 1 cube = 4 cubes).

6. Discuss the number sentences that have been created, using the correct vocabulary.

7. Repeat this activity with different numbers.

Key checks: Can the pupils use number lines or visual representation to show subtraction and explain their thinking and demonstrate understanding? Are the pupils using the key vocabulary: less, fewer, make, total, altogether, equals, subtract, minus, take away, difference between?

Extension: Encourage the pupils to make subtraction number sentences without using cubes. This can be done either verbally or they can be written down. Can they make a number sentence that subtracts a one-digit number from a two-digit number?

Support: Guide pupils with examples using one-digit numbers and emphasise using the key vocabulary: take away, subtract, less than and equals. Show thinking on number lines, as well as using objects.

Dicey addition

Strand: Number – addition and subtraction

Learning objective: To add one-digit and two-digit numbers to 20, including zero.

You will need: dice (1–12, 1–9 and 1–6), a die which includes 0, whiteboards, whiteboard pens, number lines 0–20, cubes or objects (e.g. plastic dinosaurs)

1. **Ask:** *Who knows some of their number bonds to 20? Show me a number bond to 10.* Allow time for the pupils to show you. **Say:** *Now show me a tricky number bond to 20.* Again allow time for responses.

2. Before moving on, ensure that the pupils have an understanding of number bonds to 20.

3. Write 0 on the board. **Ask:** *What do I need to add to this to make 20?* Give the pupils time to respond.

4. **Ask:** *Why? How do you know?* Encourage the pupils to explain their thinking.

5. Roll two of the dice (e.g. you might roll 5 and 8). **Ask:** *What is 5 + 8? How can we solve this?*

6. Draw a number line on the board. Start from either 5 or 8 and count on as a group until you land on 13. Discuss how you can start on either 5 or 8 when adding.

7. Roll the dice again and repeat the activity.

8. Allow the pupils to roll the dice and practise writing and solving their own number sentences.

Key checks: Do pupils understand that they can count on from either of the two numbers to make it easier for them to add? Are the pupils using the key vocabulary: number bonds, add, more, plus, make, sum, total, altogether, equals, increase?

Extension: The pupils can investigate how many different ways there are to make a number (e.g. to make 5: 3 + 2, 10 – 5, etc.). They can record their thinking in whatever way they wish, but encourage the use of number sentences with pictorial representations.

Support: Provide the pupils with a number line that is clearly marked from 0–20, as well as cubes or other objects for hands-on problem solving.

Subtraction bingo!

Strand: Number – addition and subtraction

Learning objective: To subtract one-digit and two-digit numbers to 20, including zero.

You will need: whiteboards, whiteboard pens, number line or 100 square, number lines 0–20, cubes

1. **Say:** *Today, we are going to learn more about subtraction.*

2. **Ask:** *Can anyone remember what subtraction is?* Establish that subtraction is taking one quantity away from another.

3. Ask the pupils to split their whiteboards into six sections to play bingo. They should write a different number from 0–20 in each section.

4. **Say:** *The winner is the first person to cross out all six of their numbers.*

5. Write 20 – 6 = ? on the board. **Ask:** *Who has the answer to this question on their whiteboard?* Go through why the answer is 14 together using a number line, a 100 square or concrete materials.

6. Repeat until there is a winner.

Key checks: Can the pupils explain their thinking by recording or demonstrating understanding? Are the pupils using the key vocabulary: number bonds, equals, less than, difference between, subtract, minus, take away?

Extension: Play bingo again, but this time the pupils write mathematical statements in each of the six sections on their whiteboards (e.g. 20 – 7 or 15 – 8) and you write answers on the board.

Support: Play subtraction bingo with numbers 0–10, before moving on to teen numbers. Provide the pupils with a number line that is clearly marked from 0–20, as well as cubes for hands-on problem solving.

Addition word problems

Strand: Number – addition and subtraction

Learning objective: To solve one-step addition problems.

You will need: whiteboards, whiteboard pens, number lines or 100 squares, objects

1. Write the following word problem on the board: Fred had 2 toys and his mum gave him 3 more toys. How many toys does he have altogether?

2. **Say:** *Let's see if we can work out this problem using something called 'bar modelling'. Bar modelling is when we find out what we already know and what is unknown.*

3. **Ask:** *What are the key bits of information in this question?* Invite responses.

4. As a group, agree and underline the key parts: Fred had 2 toys and his mum gave him 3 more toys. How many toys does he have altogether?

5. **Ask:** *Why are these parts important? What do they tell us?*

6. **Say:** *We know that Fred had 2 toys* (draw a bar model representing 2) *and we also know that his mum gave him 3 more toys* (draw another bar representing 3). *So, if we add 2 and 3 together we get 5* (show this with another bar underneath the 2 + 3).

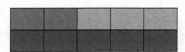

7. Repeat this activity with more word problems (e.g. 'Gita has 5 pens. Sam has 6 pens. How many pens do they have in total?' or 'Two hens lay 1 egg and 3 eggs. How many eggs altogether?').

Key checks: Do the pupils understand how the bar modelling method works? Are the pupils using the key vocabulary: plus, total of, altogether, increase by, more, combined, add, sum, together, equals, added to, in all, make?

Extension: Encourage the pupils to write their own addition word problems.

Support: Provide the pupils with a number line or 100 square to support their addition, or objects to allow hands-on thinking.

Subtraction word problems

Strand: Number – addition and subtraction

Learning objective: To solve one-step subtraction problems.

You will need: whiteboards, whiteboard pens, number lines or 100 squares, objects

1. Write the following word problem on the board: A packet has 7 sweets inside. How many sweets will be left if I eat 4?

2. **Say:** *Let's see if we can work out this problem using bar modelling.* Remind the pupils that bar modelling is when we find out what we already know and what is unknown.

3. **Ask:** *What are the key bits of information in this question?* Invite responses.

4. As a group, agree and underline the key parts: A packet has 7 sweets inside. How many sweets will be left if I eat 4?

5. **Ask:** *Why are these parts important? What do they tell us?*

6. **Say:** *We know that there are 7 sweets in the packet* (draw a bar model representing the total, which is 7) *and we know that 4 are eaten* (draw another bar underneath representing 4). *So, if we subtract 4 from 7, we get 3* (show this by adding another three boxes to the bar).

7. Repeat this activity with more word problems (e.g. 'Andy has 9 trading cards, but loses 3 of them. How many does he have now?' or 'Miroslav made 6 cakes. 3 of the cakes got eaten. How many are left?').

Key checks: Do the pupils understand how the bar modelling method works? Are the pupils using the key vocabulary: subtract, take away, decrease by, minus, shared, fewer than, less than, difference between?

Extension: Encourage the pupils to write their own subtraction word problems.

Support: Provide the pupils with a number line or 100 square to support their subtraction, or objects to allow hands-on thinking.

Addition and subtraction word problems

Strand: Number – addition and subtraction

Learning objective: To solve one-step addition and subtraction problems.

You will need: whiteboards, whiteboard pens, number lines or 100 squares, objects

1. Write the following word problem on the board: Jo has 4 books. Eve gives her 2 more. How many books does Jo have now?

2. **Say:** *Let's see if we can work out this problem using bar modelling.* Remind the pupils that bar modelling is when we find out what we already know and what is unknown.

3. **Ask:** *What are the key bits of information in this question?* Invite responses.

4. As a group, agree and underline the key parts: Jo has <u>4 books</u>. Eve gives her <u>2 more</u>. <u>How many</u> books does Jo have <u>now</u>?

5. **Ask:** *Why are these parts important? What do they tell us?*

6. **Say:** *We know that Jo had 4 books* (draw a bar model representing 4) *and we know that Eve gave her 2 more* (draw another bar representing 2). *So, if we add 4 and 2 together, we get 6* (show this underneath the 4 + 2).

7. Repeat this activity with more word problems (e.g. 'Ben has 10 marbles. He loses 7 marbles. How many marbles does he have left?' or 'Kyle has 4 hats. Ali has 5 hats. How many hats do they have altogether?')

Key checks: Do the pupils understand how the bar modelling method works and when to use addition and subtraction methods? Are the pupils using the key vocabulary: plus, total of, altogether, equals, increase by, combined, add, sum, together, more than, added to, in all, make, subtract, gave, take away, decrease by, less, fewer, minus, shared, difference between?

Extension: Ask the pupils to write their own addition and subtraction word problems.

Support: Provide the pupils with a number line or 100 square to support their addition and subtraction, or objects to allow hands-on thinking.

Colour counting

Strand: Number – multiplication and division

Learning objective: To count in multiples of twos, fives and tens.

You will need: 100 squares, different coloured counters or coloured pencils, number lines or base 10 blocks

1. Show the pupils a 100 square. Colour or place a counter on 5 and 10.

2. **Ask:** *Does anyone know why I coloured 5 and 10?* Listen to their answers.

3. **Ask:** *What do you think I will colour next?* Give the pupils time to answer.

4. Ask the pupils to continue counting in fives and to colour/place a counter on the next few numbers.

5. **Ask:** *What do you notice when you count in fives?*

6. Ask the pupils to do the same for counting in twos and tens, using a different colour for each.

7. **Ask:** *Can you see a pattern? What can you see?* (The pupils should notice that the multiplication tables have similar numbers in them, but they do not have to know all the similarities between the tables at this stage.)

8. As a group, the pupils count in twos, fives and tens but, every time they say a number that has multiple tables in it (e.g. 10), they have to clap or jump.

9. Write several numbers on the board and ask the pupils to identify which numbers are being used when we count in twos, fives or tens. Can they tell you why? (Pupils might suggest that the numbers ending in 5 and 0 are in the 5 multiplication table, numbers that end in 0 are in the 10 multiplication table and numbers that end in 0, 2, 4, 6 or 8 are in the 2 multiplication table. They may also notice the relationship between all multiplication tables.)

Key checks: Can the pupils count in twos, fives and tens without the 100 square? Are the pupils using the key vocabulary: multiple, count on, groups of, addition, multiplication, lots of?

Extension: When counting in twos, fives and tens, ask the pupils to fill in missing numbers (e.g. say 2, 4, 6 and the pupil has to state the next number). Ask the pupils to explain how they know the next number and link their explanation to odds and evens, numbers ending in 5 or 0, etc.

Support: Encourage the pupils to use a number line or a base 10 block to help support their counting.

Butterfly doubles

Strand: Number – multiplication and division

Learning objective: To double a number.

You will need: whiteboards, whiteboard pens, 1–6 and 1–9 dice

1. **Say:** *Some butterflies are 'symmetrical', which means they have the same design on both sets of wings.*

2. Draw a butterfly on the whiteboard and draw two dots on one set of wings.

3. **Ask:** *What needs to go on the other set of wings to make it symmetrical?* (two dots) *How many dots do we have altogether?* (four) *The original number of dots has doubled!*

4. **Ask:** *So, what is double two? How do you know?*

5. Repeat with five dots on one set of wings and ask the pupils if they can show you double five by drawing the butterfly with five dots on each set of wings.

6. Allow the pupils to roll a die to generate a number to double using butterflies.

Key checks: Do the pupils know what doubling means and can they show you using the butterflies? Are the pupils using the key vocabulary: double, near double, the same?

Extension: The pupils can use concrete objects to show doubles (e.g. show double three is six using counters or cubes).

Support: Encourage the pupils to look at the dots on their die. They first draw them on one side of the butterfly and then repeat this on the other side. They can then count aloud to find the answer.

Awesome arrays

Strand: Number – multiplication and division

Learning objective: To use arrays to show numbers.

You will need: a wide variety of coloured cubes, whiteboards, whiteboard pens, number lines

1. **Ask:** *Who can add 2 and 2 together? Can you show me using the cubes?*
   The pupils use the cubes to show 2 + 2 = 4.

2. **Say:** *Arrays are made when a set of objects is put into rows or columns. Each column or row must have the same number of objects as the other rows or columns.*

3. Show the pupils an array such as 2 + 2 + 2.

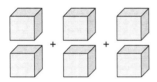

4. As a group, count all the cubes until you get to 6.

5. **Say:** *We have just multiplied! We could say 2 + 2 + 2 = 6 or that 3 times 2 is 6.*

6. Show this again with 2 + 2 + 2 or 2 × 3.

7. Encourage the pupils to use the cubes to create their own arrays. Help them to draw their arrays on their whiteboards and to write the number sentence underneath when they have made their cube model.

Key checks: Do the pupils put the numbers they are adding into arrays/rows for ease of counting? Are the pupils using the key vocabulary: array, row, column, add, together, altogether, equals, plus, sum of?

Extension: Encourage the pupils to use other materials to create arrays (e.g. pencils or counters).

Support: Provide the pupils with a number line to help them with their counting.

Multiplication problems

Strand: Number – multiplication and division

Learning objective: To solve simple multiplication problems using twos, fives and tens.

You will need: whiteboards, whiteboard pens, number lines, objects

1. Write the following word problem on the board: Jon has 2 bags of sweets. There are 10 sweets in each bag. How many sweets does Jon have in total?

2. **Say:** *Let's see if we can work out this problem using bar modelling.* Remind the pupils that bar modelling is when we find out what we already know and what is unknown.

3. **Ask:** *What are the key bits of information in this question?* Invite responses.

4. As a group, agree and underline the key parts: Jon has <u>2 bags of sweets</u>. There are <u>10 sweets in each bag</u>. <u>How many</u> sweets does Jon have <u>in total</u>?

5. **Ask:** *Why are these parts important? What do they tell us?* (that there are 2 groups with 10 in each group)

6. **Say:** *We know there are 2 bags of sweets* (draw a bar model representing 2 equal groups) *and we know there are 10 sweets in each bag* (write 10 in each section of the bar model). *So, if we add 10 and 10, we get 20.*

20	
10	10

$2 \times 10 = 20$

7. Repeat this activity with more word problems (e.g. 'Charlotte has 5 boxes of pencils. There are 6 pencils in each box. How many pencils does Charlotte have altogether?').

Key checks: Do the pupils understand how the bar modelling method works and how to work out how many groups to multiply? Are the pupils using the key vocabulary: product, multiple of, times, multiply, multiply by, total?

Extension: Ask the pupils to write their own multiplication word problems for each other to solve and check using bar modelling.

Support: Provide the pupils with number lines to support their counting and also objects for hands-on thinking. The pupils can focus on counting in twos to begin with.

Division problems

Strand: Number – multiplication and division

Learning objective: To solve simple division problems using twos, fives and tens.

You will need: whiteboards, whiteboard pens, multiplication grids/lines, objects

1. Write the following word problem on the board: Sara has 10 oranges. She wants to share half the oranges with her sister. How many do they each get?

2. **Say:** *Let's see if we can work out this problem using bar modelling.* Remind the pupils that bar modelling is when we find out what we already know and what is unknown.

3. **Ask:** *What are the key bits of information in this question?* Invite responses. As a group, agree and underline the key parts: Sara has <u>10 oranges</u>. She wants to <u>share half</u> the oranges with her sister. <u>How many</u> do they <u>each</u> get?

4. **Ask:** *Why are these parts important? What do they tell us?* (there are 10 things to be shared between 2 people)

5. **Say:** *We know that Sara has 10 oranges* (draw a bar model representing 10) *and that she wants to share half of them with her sister* (draw another bar underneath representing 2 equal groups).

6. Using equipment such as cubes, share 10 between 2 groups evenly. Or ask the pupils what relevant multiplication fact they know from the 2 multiplication table: ? × 2 = 10. (5)

10	
5	5

   $10 \div 2 = 5$

7. Repeat with more word problems (e.g. 'Sophie had 20 figs that she wanted to share between herself and 4 friends. How many did they each get?').

Key checks: Do the pupils understand how the bar modelling method works and which number should be divided? Are the pupils using the key vocabulary: half, halve, share, share equally, group in pairs, equal groups of?

Extension: Ask the pupils to write their own division word problems for each other to solve and check using bar modelling.

Support: Provide the pupils with multiplication grids/lines to support their multiplication tables and also objects for hands-on thinking.

Mixed problems

Strand: Number – multiplication and division

Learning objective: To solve simple multiplication and division problems using twos, fives and tens.

You will need: whiteboards, whiteboard pens, cubes, number lines, objects

1. Write the following word problem on the board: Jack bought 4 sweets that cost 5p each. How much did he spend altogether?

2. **Say:** *Let's see if we can work out this problem using bar modelling.*

3. **Ask:** *What are the key bits of information in this question? Is it a multiplication problem or a division problem? How do you know? Show me how you know.*

4. As a group, underline the key parts: Jack bought <u>4 sweets</u> that cost <u>5p each</u>. <u>How much</u> did he spend <u>altogether?</u>

5. **Ask:** *Why are these parts important? What do they tell us?* (there are 4 sweets and each sweet costs 5p)

6. **Say:** *We know there are 4 sweets* (draw a bar model representing 4 even groups) *and that they cost 5p each* (write 5 in each section of the bar model). *So, if we add 4 lots of 5, we get 20.* Count this together and say 4 × 5p = 20p. You could also use an array of cubes to represent the sweets.

20			
5	5	5	5

4 × 5 = 20

7. Repeat with more word problems (e.g. 'Flo has 40 grapes to share between herself and 9 friends. How many grapes each?' or 'Rachel and her 4 friends each have 2 bracelets. How many bracelets altogether?').

Key checks: Do the pupils understand how the bar modelling method works and when to use multiplication and division methods? Are the pupils using the key vocabulary: lots of, groups of, multiple of, times, multiply, multiply by, double, halve, share, share equally, group in pairs, equal groups of?

Extension: Ask the pupils to write their own multiplication and division word problems for each other to solve and check.

Support: Provide number lines for support and objects for hands-on thinking. Start with questions involving twos and build up to fives and tens.

A shape of two halves

Strand: Number – fractions

Learning objective: To understand that a half is a whole divided into two equal parts (halving shapes).

You will need: paper shapes, whiteboards, whiteboard pens, scissors, playdough, cookie cutters

1. Draw several shapes on the board (e.g. square, triangle, rectangle).

2. Draw a line on one of the shapes so that the line cuts the shape into half and then label each half with $\frac{1}{2}$. **Say:** *Two equal parts make a whole.* Show the pupils this using a paper shape that can be cut or folded.

3. Ask the pupils to draw a square on their whiteboards and to draw a line to cut it in half. Repeat with a circle and a triangle, reminding the pupils to use the language 'half'.

4. **Ask:** *What do two halves make?* Invite responses. Ensure correct language is used; **say:** *Two halves equal a whole.* You may wish to show this using a piece of paper cut or folded into halves.

5. Instruct the pupils to use cookie cutters and playdough to cut shapes in half to see the two halves.

Key checks: Can the pupils accurately fold or cut the shapes in half? Are the pupils using the key vocabulary: half, halves, whole, fold, same, equal?

Extension: The pupils can use more difficult regular shapes to find halves (e.g. hexagons, pentagons, octagons). They can find half of more than one object (e.g. half of three circles = one and a half).

Support: Provide the pupils with a variety of different-shaped 'halves' and ask them to match them to make a whole.

Half of it!

Strand: Number – fractions

Learning objective: To understand that a half is a whole divided into two equal parts (halving numbers).

You will need: whiteboards, whiteboard pens, counters, two dice or spinners with even numbers up to 20

1. Write the number 10 on a whiteboard and show the pupils 10 counters. Place the whiteboard on the table and draw a line so the number 10 is split in two.

2. **Ask:** *How could we use this whiteboard to find half of a number?* Take pupils' suggestions.

3. As a group, put one counter on each side until you get to 10 (at which point there should be 5 on each side of the whiteboard).

4. Roll two dice or use a spinner to generate a number to find half of and repeat the activity as a group.

5. Encourage the pupils to repeat this activity individually using dice or spinners to generate numbers.

Key checks: Do the pupils have the same amount on each side? Are the pupils using the key vocabulary: double, near double, half, halve, the same?

Extension: Ask the pupils to partition tens and ones to split higher numbers; encourage the use of existing number bonds.

Support: Focus on single even numbers at first to build confidence.

Feisty fractions

Strand: Number – fractions

Learning objective: To understand that a half is a whole divided into two equal parts (halving objects and quantities).

You will need: whiteboards, whiteboard pens, cubes, balance scale if required

1. Recap what a half is. **Say:** *A half is two equal parts.*

2. **Ask:** *Can you show this by drawing a shape?* Ask the pupils to draw any shape on their whiteboards. **Ask:** *Can you show me a half?* Ask the pupils to draw a line to split their shape into two halves.

3. **Say:** *Today we will be finding half of an amount or quantity.*

4. Show the pupils 16 cubes. **Ask:** *How can I find out what is half of these cubes?* Invite responses. **Say:** *We can put them into two groups because to make a half we divide things into two equal groups.*

5. Show the pupils how to split the 16 cubes by putting one cube at a time into each half of a whiteboard with a line drawn down it until there are 8 on each side. **Say:** *Half of 16 is 8 or 8 is half of 16.*

6. As a group, repeat this activity with 22 cubes. Together **say:** *11 is half of 22 or half of 22 is 11.*

7. Allow the pupils time to practise further problems independently and take note of who can use the above strategy.

Key checks: Can the pupils accurately group the cubes? Are the pupils using the key vocabulary: half, halves, same, equal?

Extension: Ask the pupils what strategy they would use for numbers above 20. Which part of the number would they explore first (tens or ones), and why? Can the pupils show halving in different contexts (e.g. money)?

Support: Use smaller numbers for the pupils to investigate. Allow the pupils to keep a tally mark in each section to ensure they are counting accurately. Perhaps use a balance scale with identical objects on each side, explaining that you need the same amount on each side to balance and that each pan holds half of the total.

Shape quarters

Strand: Number – fractions

Learning objective: To understand that a quarter is a whole divided into four equal parts.

You will need: whiteboards, whiteboard pens, paper shapes, scissors

1. Draw several shapes on the board (e.g. square, diamond, rectangle).

2. Draw two lines on one of the shapes so that the lines cut the shape into quarters and then label each quarter with $\frac{1}{4}$.

3. Show this using a paper shape that can be cut or folded. **Say:** *Four quarters make a whole.*

4. Ask the pupils to draw a square and do the same. Repeat with a circle and a rhombus, reminding the pupils to use the language 'quarter'.

5. **Ask:** *What do four quarters make?* Invite responses.

6. **Say:** *Four quarters equal a whole.* You may wish to show this using a piece of paper cut or folded into quarters.

7. Encourage the pupils to draw shapes (e.g. squares, rectangles, circles), split them into quarters and write $\frac{1}{4}$ in each section.

Key checks: Are the pupils accurately folding, cutting and labelling the shapes? Are the pupils using the key vocabulary: quarter, whole, same, equal?

Extension: The pupils can find quarters of more complex shapes (e.g. regular hexagons, octagons).

Support: Provide the pupils with a variety of quarters of shapes and ask them to match them up to make complete shapes.

Quantity quarters

Strand: Number – fractions

Learning objective: To find a quarter of shapes, objects and quantities.

You will need: whiteboards, whiteboard pens, paper shapes, scissors, cubes

1. Recap what a quarter is. Ask the pupils to draw a square on their whiteboards. **Ask:** *Can you show me a quarter?*

2. Also show this using a paper shape that can be cut or folded.

3. Ask the pupils to split their whiteboard into four quarters.

4. **Say:** *In this session, you will be finding a quarter of an amount or quantity.*

5. Show the pupils 12 cubes. **Ask:** *How can I find a quarter of these cubes?* Invite responses. **Say:** *We can put them into four groups.*

6. Show the pupils how to split the 12 cubes by putting one cube at a time into each quarter of a whiteboard until there are three in each quarter. **Say:** *A quarter of 12 is 3 or 3 is a quarter of 12.*

7. As a group, repeat this activity with 24 cubes. Together **say:** *6 is a quarter of 24 or a quarter of 24 is 6.*

8. Give the pupils time to practise further problems independently and take note of who can use the above strategy.

Key checks: Can the pupils accurately group the cubes? Are the pupils using the key vocabulary: shape, quarter, split, share, divide, quantity, amount, group, equally?

Extension: Ask the pupils to complete a quartering wall.

16			
8		8	
4	4	4	4

Support: Allow the pupils to find quarters of simple numbers to start with (e.g. 4, 8, 12, 16) to build their confidence.

Tallest and shortest

Strand: Measurement – comparing and estimating

Learning objective: To compare and describe lengths using words such as long, short, tall.

You will need: whiteboards, whiteboard pens, string, objects in the classroom

1. **Say:** *Today you will be learning about length.*

2. **Ask:** *Can you all line up in height order?* Observe how the pupils line up.

3. **Ask:** *Who is at the front? Why?* (Because they are the tallest or the shortest; if this vocabulary is not used, ensure that you model its use.)

4. **Say:** *So* (name) *is the tallest and* (name) *is the shortest.*

5. **Say:** *We could say that* (name) *is 1st,* (name) *is 2nd, and so on.*

6. Ask the pupils to name and write on their whiteboards three objects that are taller than they are (e.g. a door, a bookshelf, a lamp post).

7. Repeat the activity for objects that are shorter than they are.

Key checks: Can the pupils explain their thoughts about length and clearly explain the difference between shortest and tallest/longest? Are the pupils using the key vocabulary: long, longer, longest, short, shorter, shortest, tall, taller, tallest?

Extension: The pupils could independently use a length of string and find objects in the classroom that are longer or shorter than it.

Support: Allow the pupils to work with extremes; for example, compare a pencil with a chair using the vocabulary short, tall, shorter and taller.

How many cubes?

Strand: Measurement – comparing and estimating

Learning objective: To measure and begin to record lengths using non-standard units.

You will need: whiteboards, whiteboard pens, objects in the classroom (e.g. pencils, gluesticks, rulers, metre ruler), cubes, centimetre rulers

1. Recap the meaning of shortest and tallest.

2. **Say:** *Today we are going to estimate.*

3. **Ask:** *Does anyone know what 'estimate' means?* Take pupils' responses.

4. **Say:** *Estimate means 'to make a sensible guess'.*

5. Put an object on the table (e.g. a pencil), together with some cubes.

6. **Ask:** *How many cubes long do you think the pencil is?*

7. Prompt the pupils to write their 'guestimate' on their whiteboards.

8. Now measure the pencil with the cubes.

9. Ask the pupils to 'guestimate' the length of the other objects and to record their 'guestimates' on their whiteboards.

10. Ask the pupils to measure objects using different units (e.g. pencils or gluesticks rather than cubes).

Key checks: Can the pupils demonstrate their understanding of length by comparing different objects? Can they explain their guestimates? Are the pupils using the key vocabulary: long, longer, longest, short, shorter, shortest?

Extension: The pupils can begin to use a centimetre ruler to estimate and measure to the nearest centimetre.

Support: Allow the pupils to physically hold measuring tools (e.g. a cube) so that they can understand the length of one unit to help them estimate. Get the pupils to order the size of the individual objects, using key vocabulary such as larger and smaller. Then move on to measuring the objects with cubes.

Measuring in metres

Strand: Measurement – comparing and estimating

Learning objective: To measure lengths using manageable standard units (e.g. metres).

You will need: whiteboards, whiteboard pens, gluesticks, metre rulers, string

1. **Say:** *Today we will be learning more about estimating and measuring.*

2. Recap estimation with the pupils.

3. **Ask:** *How long is a metre? Is it longer than a bed? A desk? A cricket bat?*

4. **Ask:** *How many pens will fit end to end into one metre?*

5. **Ask:** *How many gluesticks will fit end to end into a metre?*

6. **Say:** *Today you will be finding objects that are different lengths. You will put the objects you find into three lists: less than one metre, about one metre and more than one metre.* Model lists with these headings on the board.

Less than one metre	About one metre	More than one metre

7. Provide time for pupils to walk around the classroom and find objects to add to each list.

8. **Ask:** *Which of the objects you have chosen should be measured in centimetres? Which should be measured in metres?* As a group, list objects that should be measured in centimetres and metres.

9. Repeat the exercise and estimate objects that are 10 cm.

Key checks: Can the pupils explain which item is longer and why they know this? Can they explain their guestimates? Are the pupils using the key vocabulary: long, longer, longest, short, shorter, shortest, metre, centimetre?

Extension: Provide the pupils with a metre ruler and a piece of string measuring more than one metre. Ensure the string is curled to 'look' the same as one metre. **Ask:** *Which is longer – the string or the ruler? Explain your reasoning.*

Support: Provide the pupils with a metre ruler to help them gather objects and focus on estimating metres and measuring in metres.

Mass learning

Strand: Measurement – comparing and estimating

Learning objective: To compare and describe mass using words such as heavier and lighter.

You will need: whiteboards, whiteboard pens, objects with different mass (e.g. pencils, books, gluesticks, cubes), weighing/balance scales

1. **Say:** *Today we are going to learn about mass.*

2. Show the pupils two objects that very obviously have a different mass (e.g. a pencil and a book).

3. **Ask:** *What can you tell me about these two objects? What words could you use to describe them?*

4. **Ask:** *Which one do you think is heavier? How can we work out which object is heavier?* Listen to the pupils' suggestions. Then suggest that we could be weighing scales and use our hands.

5. Ask one pupil to close their eyes. Place one object in either hand. They have to act like a scale and show or say which object is heavier and which is lighter.

6. Allow time for all the pupils to take part in this activity. Encourage language such as heavier, lighter, heavier than, lighter than.

7. **Ask:** *Can you draw a picture to show which object is heavier?*

Key checks: Can the pupils explain their thoughts about mass (e.g. which item is the heaviest or lightest and why)? Can they give reasons linked to key vocabulary? Are the pupils using the key vocabulary: mass, weigh, weighs, balances, heavy, heavier, heaviest, light, lighter, lightest?

Extension: Ask the pupils what is the heaviest thing they can think of and what is the lightest thing they can think of. Compare all the suggestions and discuss which would be the heaviest or lightest of all.

Support: Provide the pupils with an object to hold when comparing other objects or use balance scales to see the difference between two objects.

Unbalanced

Strand: Measurement – comparing and estimating

Learning objective: To measure and begin to record mass using non-standard units.

You will need: weighing/balance scales, classroom objects to weigh (e.g. gluesticks, pencils, books), a variety of small toys

1. **Say:** *Today you will be learning about mass and how to measure objects using a balance scale.*

2. Let the pupils feel the weight of a gluestick and then the weight of a cube (wooden cubes would be better than multi-link cubes).

3. **Ask:** *How many cubes do you think the gluestick weighs?* Record their 'guestimates'.

4. Introduce the term 'trial and error' and explain that nobody is 'wrong'; we are all just investigating.

5. As a group, place the gluestick on one side of the balance scale, then put in one cube at a time on the other side and count aloud. As a group, state that one gluestick weighs __ cubes.

6. Repeat with a variety of objects.

7. Ask the pupils to place the objects you have used in order. Let them choose which order to use and ask them to tell you how the objects have been ordered – heaviest to lightest or lightest to heaviest.

Key checks: Can the pupils explain their thoughts about mass (e.g. which item is the heaviest or lightest and why)? Can they suggest another way to weigh, rather than using the balance scales? Are the pupils using the key vocabulary: mass, weigh, weighs, balances, heavy, heavier, heaviest, light, lighter, lightest?

Extension: Place two different objects on each side of a balance scale. **Ask:** *What would happen if we had two of one of the objects? Explain your reasoning.* Hang stockings from a hook and place objects in them to see which weighs more (i.e. which stretches the stocking the most).

Support: The pupils could balance significantly differently weighted objects to demonstrate the difference between them.

Hunting for treasure

Strand: Measurement – comparing and estimating

Learning objective: To measure mass using manageable standard units.

You will need: weighing/balance scales, objects that weigh less than and more than 1kg, a variety of 1kg objects (e.g. a 1kg weight, a bag of sugar/flour/pasta)

1. **Say:** *Today you will be looking at mass.* **Ask:** *What is measured in kilograms? Invite responses.*

2. **Say:** *We measure solids in grams and kilograms, but we usually measure liquids in millilitres and litres.*

3. Display the 1kg weights and objects. Encourage the pupils to handle them and place them on the scales to compare and see equal mass.

4. **Say:** *You are going to try to find items in the classroom or playground that have a mass of about 1kg.*

5. The pupils find and record items which they estimate have a mass of 1kg.

6. As a group, the pupils use the scales and record whether their objects have a mass of 1kg, more than 1kg or less than 1kg.

Key checks: Can the pupils explain their thoughts about mass (e.g. which item is the heaviest or lightest and why)? Can the pupils suggest another way to weigh, rather than using the scales? Are the pupils using the key vocabulary: mass, weigh, weighs, balances, heavy, heavier, heaviest, light, lighter, lightest, kilogram, grams?

Extension: Repeat the activity, but this time look for objects with a mass of 500g.

Support: Provide the pupils with a 1kg bag of sugar so that they can physically compare this mass to help them classify other objects as heavier, lighter or the same in a Venn diagram.

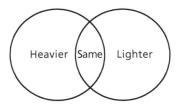

Empty or full?

Strand: Measurement – comparing and estimating

Learning objective: To compare and describe capacity using words such as empty, full, less than half and full.

You will need: a variety of containers (some the same, some different), a source of water, containers with half full marked

1. **Say:** *Today you will be learning about capacity.*

2. **Ask:** *Does anyone know what capacity is?* Invite responses.

3. **Say:** *Capacity is the amount that something can hold.*

4. Show the pupils four identical containers with water in them: one full, one half full, one a quarter full and one empty. Discuss which contains the most water and which contains the least water.

5. **Ask:** *How could we label each of these containers?* Take pupils' suggestions.

6. Label each container as full, half full, a quarter full and empty.

7. Provide each pupil with a container (preferably all the same shape).

8. **Ask:** *Can you show me half full or half empty? Why are these two things the same?*

9. Repeat with quarter full and full.

Key checks: Can the pupils explain their thoughts about capacity (e.g. which container contains the most or least and why)? Are the pupils using the key vocabulary: empty, full, half full, half empty, quarter full, capacity, container, measure, most, least?

Extension: Repeat the above activity using different shaped containers.

Support: Provide the pupils with containers that have marked lines to show half full.

Guestimate

Strand: Measurement – comparing and estimating

Learning objective: To measure and begin to record capacity using non-standard units.

You will need: a variety of containers of different sizes, a small container (e.g. a small yoghurt pot), a source of water or rice/sand, a one-litre measuring jug

1. **Ask:** *Can anyone remember what capacity is?* **Say:** *Capacity is the amount that something can hold.*

2. Show the pupils a variety of different containers and the yoghurt pot. Ask them to choose one of the larger containers to start with.

3. **Ask:** *How many yoghurt pots of water/rice/sand do you think we will need to fill this container?* Encourage the pupils to respond with their estimates.

4. **Ask:** *How can we find out?* Invite responses.

5. On the board, write:

Container	Guestimate	How many filled it up?	Estimate correct?

6. As a group, count how many yoghurt pots of water/rice/sand fill the container and complete the table. Discuss the results and see if anyone made a good guess.

7. Repeat this activity with different containers. Label the containers A, B, C, etc.

8. Discuss which container holds the most and which holds the least.

Key checks: Can the pupils explain their thoughts about capacity (e.g. which container holds the most/least and why)? Are the pupils using the key vocabulary: empty, full, half/quarter/three-quarters full, capacity, volume, measure, most, least?

Extension: The pupils can begin to measure in litres, using the correct language to describe the capacity of a container.

Support: The adult orders the containers from smallest to largest capacity before beginning. Focus on the 'How many filled it up?' column in the table to start with so that pupils have a point of reference. Then begin estimating, once understanding is shown.

Litres and millilitres

Strand: Measurement – comparing and estimating

Learning objective: To measure capacity using manageable standard units (litres).

You will need: a one-litre water bottle, a variety of containers with no measuring lines (different sizes, including at least one with a capacity of more than one litre), a one-litre measuring jug, a source of water, whiteboards, whiteboard pens, a 500mL bottle

1. **Ask:** *Can anyone remember what capacity is?* Invite responses.

2. **Say:** *Capacity is the amount that something can hold.*

3. **Ask:** *What is your favourite drink?* Allow the pupils time to respond.

4. **Say:** *We buy lots of our drinks and measure them in litres, like this* (show a one-litre water bottle). *This bottle holds one litre of water.*

5. **Ask:** *What else can we buy in one-litre bottles?* Invite responses.

6. Show the pupils the different containers. **Ask:** *Do you think any of these containers can hold one litre?*

7. Label the containers A, B, C, etc. Ask the pupils to write on their whiteboards which containers they think will hold a litre and which they think will hold more or less than a litre. Model the use of a table to record their thinking.

Container	Estimate	Estimate correct?
A	More than 1 litre	
B	1 litre	

8. As a group, fill the containers with water and then pour the water into the one-litre measuring jug to see if the pupils' estimates were correct.

9. Discuss which container holds the most water and which holds the least water.

Key checks: Can the pupils explain their thoughts about capacity (e.g. which container holds the most or least and why)? Are the pupils using the key vocabulary: empty, full, half full, quarter full, three-quarters full, capacity, volume, container, measure, most, least, millilitres, litres, mL, L?

Extension: Introduce 500mL or 0.5 litres using a soft drink bottle and ask the pupils to predict if any of the containers have a capacity of 500mL or half a litre.

Support: Provide a variety of examples of one litre in different containers to physically show one litre.

Days and months

Strand: Measurement – time

Learning objective: To know the days of the week and months of the year.

You will need: whiteboards, whiteboard pens, a calendar

1. **Ask:** *How many days are in a week? Can you name them?*

2. As a group, chant the days of the week. Clap twice then say 'Monday', clap twice then say 'Tuesday', etc.

3. **Ask:** *What day was yesterday? What day is tomorrow?*

4. **Ask:** *What month is your birthday in?* Ask the pupils to respond and then to line up in month of birthday order.

5. **Ask:** *Now that we know some of the months of the year, can you tell me how many months are in a year? Can you name them all?*

6. As a group, chant the months of the year. Jump and clap then say 'January', jump and clap then say 'February', etc.

7. **Ask:** *What month comes after January? What is the last month of the year?* Ask similar questions.

Key checks: Check the pupils' understanding by asking questions (e.g. 'What is the month after June?'). Are the pupils using the key vocabulary: days of the week (Monday, Tuesday, etc.), months of the year (January, February, etc.), seasons (spring, summer, autumn, winter), day, week, month, year?

Extension: Ask the pupils to put the months of the year into seasons on their whiteboards.

Support: Provide the pupils with a calendar so they can see the days and months and pictorial images linked to each month. The pupils can use this to check that the group has ordered itself correctly in birthday month order.

Logical order

Strand: Measurement – time

Learning objective: To sequence events in logical order.

You will need: whiteboards, whiteboard pens, paper, pencils, pictures of daily events

1. **Say:** *Today we are going to learn about sequencing and doing things in a logical order.*

2. **Say:** *This morning I got up, put my pyjamas on, drank some orange juice, and then ate breakfast. Does that sound right to you? Why not?*

3. **Say:** *We do things in a logical order so that they make sense.*

4. Write the following events on the board: end of school, lunchtime, playtime, registration, wake up, breakfast.

5. **Ask:** *Can you write these events in a logical order? What order do they happen in during the day?*

6. Ask one pupil to instruct you how to make breakfast by giving the logical sequence of events and using suitable language (e.g. first get the cereal, next put it in a bowl, then add milk, then eat it).

7. Ask the pupils to take turns in instructing each other how to make a sandwich or brush their teeth.

Key checks: Do the pupils understand the phrase 'logical order'? Can they give examples of events done in logical order? Are the pupils using the key vocabulary: first, second, third, last, before, after, logical, sequence, order?

Extension: The pupils draw a poster that shows events during the day from waking up (top left) to going to bed (bottom right).

Support: Provide images of daily events for the pupils to sequence.

O'clock and half past

Strand: Measurement – time

Learning objective: To tell the time (o'clock and half past).

You will need: analogue clocks with moveable hands, whiteboards, whiteboard pens, blank bingo cards divided into six sections, pencils

1. Show the pupils an analogue clock displaying 12 o'clock.

2. **Ask:** *Does anyone know what time this clock is showing?*

3. **Say:** *The long hand shows the minutes and the short hand shows the hour. This clock is showing 12 o'clock.*

4. Repeat with one o'clock and two o'clock. Ask the pupils to show the times on their own clocks by moving the hands.

5. Show the pupils half past one on the clock. **Ask:** *Does anyone know what time this clock is showing?*

6. **Say:** *The long hand shows the minutes, which in this case shows half past, and the short hand shows the hour. This clock is showing half past one.*

7. As a group, show half past three and half past six. Ensure the pupils can see the difference between half past and o'clock times.

8. Ask the pupils to write six times on a blank bingo card (e.g. one o'clock, half past four, three o'clock, half past five).

9. Show the pupils a time using the clock. The pupils cross out the times on their bingo cards if they have them. The first pupil to cross out all six of their times shouts 'Bingo!' and is the winner.

Key checks: Can the pupils read the clock correctly, differentiating between the big and small hands? Are the pupils using the key vocabulary: hour, minutes, o'clock, half past, clock, watch, hands, hour hand, minute hand?

Extension: The pupils state what time events happen during the school day (e.g. playtime, lunch, home time).

Support: The pupils concentrate on o'clock times only at first and move on to half past when ready.

Name that shape

Strand: Geometry – properties of shapes

Learning objective: To name and describe common 2-D shapes.

You will need: 2-D shapes (squares, rectangles, triangles and circles), 3-D shapes (cubes, cuboids, triangular- and square-based pyramids, cones), bag

1. **Say:** *Today you will be exploring 2-D shapes.*

2. **Ask:** *Can anyone name a 2-D shape?* Take pupils' responses.

3. **Say:** *2-D shapes are flat and we cannot pick them up! 2-D shapes are used to make 3-D shapes.* Show pupils some examples of 3-D shapes containing 2-D shapes.

4. Show the pupils a square. **Ask:** *What is the name of this shape?* Invite responses. Then tell them it is called a square.

5. **Ask:** *How would you describe this shape*? Encourage the pupils to describe the square (e.g. four straight sides, four vertices, four sides are equal in length).

6. Repeat this activity for the rectangle, triangle and circle.

7. Place all the 2-D shapes in a bag and model describing a shape to the pupils (e.g. 'This shape has three vertices and three sides. What could it be? A triangle').

8. Each pupil takes a turn to feel a shape in the bag and describe it to the other pupils, who then try to name the shape.

Key checks: Do the pupils compare the vertices, sizes and sides of the shapes? Are the pupils using the key vocabulary: 2-D shape, square, rectangle, circle, triangle, vertices, sides, straight, curved?

Extension: Show the pupils 2-D shapes in different orientations and ask them to identify and describe their properties.

Support: Provide the pupils with 3-D solids and ask them to explore the 2-D shapes they can see. Then move onto the properties of 2-D shapes.

Shape discovery

Strand: Geometry – properties of shapes

Learning objective: To visualise and describe 2-D shapes.

You will need: sand (a sandpit would be ideal), 2-D shapes of varying sizes (squares, triangles, rectangles and circles)

1. **Say:** *Today you will be exploring 2-D shapes in more detail.*

2. Recap the names of common 2-D shapes and how to describe them.

3. Show the pupils the sand with parts of each shape sticking out.

4. **Ask:** *What can you see?* Encourage the pupils to respond with their ideas (e.g. shapes in the sand).

5. Point to one of the shapes and **ask:** *Which 2-D shape is this? How do you know? Convince me.*

6. Encourage the pupils to describe and name the shape (e.g. 'I can see two vertices and two sides that are the same length – it's a rectangle.').

7. Repeat this activity several times so that the pupils can see the shapes in different orientations.

Key checks: Are the pupils comparing the vertices, sizes and sides of the shapes? Are the pupils using the key vocabulary: 2-D shape, square, rectangle, circle, triangle, vertices, sides, straight, curved?

Extension: Give the pupils a variety of shapes and **ask:** *What is the same? Is there anything different about these shapes?*

Support: Start with the shapes not in the sandpit and ask the pupils to describe what they see before moving onto partially submerged shapes.

3-D properties

Strand: Geometry – properties of shapes

Learning objective: To name and describe common 3-D shapes.

You will need: 3-D shapes (cuboids, cubes, triangular- and square-based pyramids, spheres, cylinders, pentagonal-based pyramids), marker pen, bag

1. **Say:** *Today you will be exploring 3-D shapes.*

2. **Ask:** *Can anyone name a 3-D shape?* Take pupils' responses.

3. Show the pupils a cube. **Ask:** *What is the name of this shape?* Invite responses. Then tell them that it is called a cube.

4. **Ask:** *How would you describe this shape?* Listen as pupils describe the cube. **Say:** *This 3-D shape has six 'faces'.* With a pen, mark each face and count the six faces together. **Say:** *A cube has six faces. Can you see that all the faces on the cube are square?*

5. Repeat this activity with the cuboid, pyramids and sphere.

6. Place all the shapes in a bag and model describing a shape to the pupils (e.g. 'This shape has six faces, some are square and some are rectangles – it's a cuboid.').

7. Each pupil takes a turn to feel a shape in the bag and describe it to the other pupils.

Key checks: Do the pupils compare the corners, sizes, vertices and faces of the shapes? Are the pupils using the key vocabulary: 3-D shape, 2-D shape, sphere, cube, cuboid, pyramid, square, rectangle, circle, triangle, vertices, sides, flat, straight, curved?

Extension: Encourage the pupils to use more complex shapes (e.g. a cylinder or a pentagonal-based pyramid).

Support: The pupils should focus on cubes and cuboids to begin with.

3-D shape hunt

Strand: Geometry – properties of shapes

Learning objective: To visualise and describe 3-D shapes.

You will need: 3-D shapes (cuboids, cubes, cylinder, triangular- or square-based pyramids, spheres), whiteboards, whiteboard pens

1. **Say:** *Today you will be exploring 3-D shapes in more detail.*

2. Recap the names of common 3-D shapes and how to describe them (e.g. a cylinder has one rectangular face and two circular faces).

3. **Ask:** *Can anyone name a 3-D shape that is in this room?* Prompt the pupils to name a cube, cuboid, cylinder, sphere or pyramid that they can see (e.g. a globe or a box).

4. **Say:** *3-D shapes are all around us. A football is a sphere; a baked beans tin is a cylinder. Can you think of any more 3-D shapes?*

5. Tell the pupils to draw the following table on their whiteboards.

cube	cuboid	cylinder	sphere	pyramid

6. Ask the pupils to explore the room (or school if allowed) and make a note of any real-life 3-D objects under the correct heading in their tables.

7. When the pupils return, go through each shape and **ask:** *Why is this a (shape)? How do you know? Can you describe it?*

Key checks: Do the pupils compare the vertices, sizes, edges and faces of the shapes? Are the pupils using the key vocabulary: 3-D shape, 2-D shape, sphere, cube, cuboid, pyramid, square, rectangle, circle, triangle, vertices, sides, flat, straight, curved?

Extension: The pupils could create a list of 3-D shapes in the real world (e.g. buildings, sports equipment), making sure they describe the properties of the shapes.

Support: Focus on cuboids to begin with and then progress to cubes. Discuss the properties of each shape one at a time, giving plenty of opportunity to handle the shapes.

I'm spinning around

Strand: Geometry – position and direction

Learning objective: To make whole, half and quarter turns.

You will need: 2-D shapes, whiteboards, whiteboard pens, a guide showing a whole, half and quarter turn

1. Draw an arrow pointing up on the board.

2. **Ask:** *If I turn the arrow clockwise a quarter turn, which way will the arrow be facing?* You may need to discuss clockwise and explain that this is the way the hands move around the clock.

3. Show the pupils the arrow following a quarter turn.

4. Repeat with a half turn, three-quarter turn and full turn.

5. Choose a 2-D shape and draw the outline on the board.

6. Rotate the shape using the vocabulary of clockwise and quarter turns. Each time **ask:** *How many quarter turns clockwise has the shape turned?*

7. Ask the pupils to choose a shape and draw turns on their whiteboards as they explore this concept.

Key checks: Are the pupils able to draw the direction of turn on their whiteboards? Do they know what clockwise is? Are the pupils using the key vocabulary: position, direction, clockwise, turn, quarter turn, half turn, three-quarter turn, full turn?

Extension: The pupils instruct each other to turn using the correct vocabulary.

Support: Provide the pupils with a guide showing a whole, half and quarter turn. Place a 2-D shape in the original position above the guide and turn a second shape. In this way, the pupils can view the changes.

Teacherbot 3000

Strand: Geometry – position and direction

Learning objective: To describe position, direction and movement, including whole, half, quarter and three-quarter turns.

You will need: whiteboards, whiteboard pens, a sheet showing clockwise (This activity can be done inside or outside, ensuring safety.)

1. **Say:** *Today you will be controlling the Teacherbot 3000 (that's me!) using the vocabulary forwards, backwards, left, right, up, down and clockwise.*

2. Write forwards, backwards, left, right, up, down, clockwise on the board. **Ask:** *Do you know what all these words mean?* **Say:** *Clockwise is the direction that the hands move on the clock.*

3. **Say:** *I would like you to guide me around the room without bumping me into anything. You must be very clear with your instructions. You will need to tell me how many steps forward, how many turns in which direction and whether you want me to make a quarter turn, half turn, full turn and so on.*

4. Encourage the pupils to direct you safely around the room and back to the start.

5. **Say:** *Now it is time for you to be the Studentbot 3000. You will take it in turns to guide each other safely around the room.*

6. Listen for the use of key vocabulary.

Key checks: Are pupils able to use the key vocabulary to direct people around the room? Do they know what clockwise means? Are the pupils using the key vocabulary: position, direction, clockwise, turn, quarter turn, half turn, full turn, forwards, backwards, left, right, up, down?

Extension: The pupils draw a maze and write instructions to guide someone through the maze.

Support: Display a sheet that shows clockwise.

IMPACT Intervention

English Activities

How many in 30 seconds?

Strand: Reading – word reading

Learning objective: To respond speedily with the correct sound to graphemes.

You will need: flashcards of the phonemes already taught and one new one, whiteboards, whiteboard pens, a timer, a sound mat

1. Show the pupils the flashcards of the phonemes that have already been taught.

2. **Say:** *Let's see how many sounds you can say in 30 seconds. I'm going to give the cards a shuffle. Now I'm going to set the timer for 30 seconds. Ready, steady, go!*

3. Show the pupils each flashcard and ask them to tell you the sound. Place the flashcard face down on the table if the pupils are confident or place it at the back of the pack to be re-used if the pupils hesitate or say an incorrect sound.

4. **Say:** *I can't believe how many sounds you know!* Make a note of how many sounds the pupils got correct and tell them their score.

5. **Say:** *Now let's learn a new sound.* Write a new sound on the whiteboard. **Ask:** *What does this sound say*? Pupils repeat the sound. **Say:** *This is how you write the sound.* Write the letters again on the whiteboard and say the sound as you write them. **Ask:** *What sound do these letters make?*

6. **Say:** *Get your magic pen out of your invisible pocket.* **Ask:** *Can you write the new sound in the air? Can you write it again, but this time smaller, on the palm of your hand? Can you write it one more time (still with your magic finger) on your fingertip? Say the sound as you are writing it. Now get your whiteboard and write the new sound three times, big, middle-sized and small.*

Key checks: Are the pupils able to read the sounds instantly?

Extension: Provide a sound mat, which shows the sounds next to each other rather than on individual flashcards. Point to the sounds randomly so the pupils do not get used to a particular order.

Support: Go through the flashcards saying each one and asking the pupils to repeat each one before you do the timed activity.

Sound it out

Strand: Reading – word reading

Learning objective: To apply phonic knowledge as the main strategy to decode words.

You will need: 10 flashcards with individual words matching the pupils' reading ability, reading books

1. **Say:** *I'd like you to read the words on my flashcards. You are going to look for the friendly letters first.*

2. Show a flashcard (e.g. train). **Ask:** *What are the friendly letters, the two letters that make one sound?* (ai) Invite responses.

3. Point to each sound and **say** each sound in turn: *t-r-ai-n, train.* Ask the pupils to repeat it after you.

4. Repeat this process with the other flashcards, each time asking the pupils to identify the friendly letters, sound out the sounds and then blend the sounds and say the word.

5. Place two of the flashcards next to each other. **Ask:** *Can you read both words quickly? If you need to sound out the words that is fine.*

6. Continue to add extra words until all the flashcards are laid out and the pupils can read them all without sounding out the sounds.

Key checks: Do the pupils know the sounds? Are the pupils able to recognise the friendly letters?

Extension: Ask the pupils to use the same strategy to decode words in their reading books.

Support: Sound out fewer words to begin with.

Alien language

Strand: Reading – word reading

Learning objective: To read unfamiliar words by blending the sounds.

You will need: flashcards with 'alien' words on them written in lower case letters (an alien word is a nonsense word, but the sounds can be blended, e.g. 'dreb' or 'threlp')

1. **Say:** *I'm going to show you some alien words. They make no sense to humans, so they won't sound right.*

2. **Say:** *Just like words in English, I'd like you to look for the friendly letters first, and say the sounds in order, before you blend the word.*

3. Show a flashcard (e.g. 'queb'). **Ask:** *What are the friendly letters?* (qu) Invite responses.

4. Point to each sound and **say** each sound in turn: *qu-e-b, queb.* Ask the pupils to repeat the word after you.

5. Repeat this process with the other flashcards, each time asking the pupils to identify the friendly letters, sound out the sounds and then blend the sounds and say the word.

Key checks: Do the pupils know the sounds? Are the pupils able to recognise the friendly letters?

Extension: Mix up real words and alien words and ask the pupils to read them and sort them into two piles.

Support: Use words with fewer sounds to start with.

Lousy letters

Strand: Reading – word reading

Learning objective: To fluently read common exception words.

You will need: a set of flashcards showing 10 common exception words taken from your school's phonics programme or from the list in Appendix 1 of the National Curriculum (the, a, do, to, today, of, said, says, are, were, was, is, his, kind, has, I, you, your, they, be, he, me, she, we, no, go, so, by, my, here, there, where, love, come, some, one, once, ask, friend, school, put, push, pull, full, house, our)

1. **Say:** *Each of the words we are going to look at today contains a 'lousy letter' or 'lousy letters' that do not follow our rules. We are going to learn to read these words without blending them.*

2. **Ask:** *What are the 'lousy letters' in this word?* Show the pupils a flashcard (e.g. kind) and invite responses.

3. **Say:** *The lousy letter is 'i' because we would expect it to be a short 'i' sound, but it isn't.* Without sounding it out and blending, **say:** *kind.* Ask the pupils to repeat it after you.

4. Repeat this process with the other words.

5. Turn all the flashcards face down and pick up three. Hide these in your hand and flash them at the pupils in random order and ask them to say the word. Repeat each word a few times, getting faster.

6. **Ask:** *Does anyone want to be the teacher and flash the words?* Select a pupil who will choose three different words and flash them.

Key checks: Can the pupils identify the letter or letters which are the lousy letters?

Extension: Work with a greater number of words in each session.

Support: Work with fewer words. Make sure you still flash the words quickly so the pupils are reading without blending.

Let's have a lot!

Strand: Reading – word reading

Learning objective: To read words with –s or –es endings to show the plural.

You will need: flashcards for flower, chair, spoon, book, tree, glass, buzz, star, light, cup, witch, flashcards showing endings –s and –es

1. **Say:** *When they start to read, children sometimes miss the endings of words. Today we are going to look carefully at the endings of words.*

2. **Say:** *Extra letters added to the end of a word can change the meaning slightly. We are going to learn what happens when –s or –es is added.*

3. **Ask:** *Can you read these words?* Show: flower, chair, spoon, book, tree, glass. If the pupils need to be reminded of strategies, remind them to look for friendly letters first.

4. **Say:** *Each of these words is just one of each object, a single object. We call one of something the 'singular'. More than one of each object is called the 'plural'.* **Ask:** *Can you explain what the words 'singular' and 'plural' mean?*

5. **Say:** *We add –s or –es to the end of a noun to show there is more than one. So, flower becomes flowers.* Show the flashcard with the correct ending –s.

6. **Ask:** *Can you say what chair will become when it is plural?* Repeat with the other words, showing the correct ending each time.

7. **Ask:** *How do you know whether to add –s or –es?* Display these words: flower, chair, spoon, book, tree, glass.

8. **Say:** *We add –s to most words, but words that already end in s need to have –es added to turn them from singular to plural.* Show that glass needs the –es ending.

9. Show the words: buzz, star, light, cup, witch. **Ask:** *Can you say if –s or –es will need to be added to change these singular nouns to the plural ones?*

10. **Ask:** *Do we need to improve our spelling rule?* Invite responses, then **say:** *Words that have an extra syllable when they are plurals also add –es.*

Key checks: Do the pupils understand the difference between singular and plural? Do the pupils know what a noun is?

Extension: Pupils find singular and plural words in books.

Support: Draw pictures or use objects to show singular and plural.

Say and clap

Strand: Reading – word reading

Learning objective: To read multi-syllabic words.

You will need: 10–15 flashcards showing words with one, two or three syllables

1. **Say:** *To help us read words, we can split them up into syllables.*

2. **Say:** *Syllable.* Ask the pupils to repeat the word after you.

3. **Say:** *Every word has one or more syllables in it. A syllable is the number of beats or claps in a word.*

4. Demonstrate by saying and clapping the syllables in the following words. **Say:** *I want you to repeat each word after me: mum* (clap), *father* (clap clap), *playtime* (clap clap), *timetable* (clap clap clap).

5. **Ask:** *How many syllables are in the word 'mum'? How many in 'father'? How many in 'timetable'?*

6. Show the pupils the flashcards. **Ask:** *Can you sort these words into one-, two- and three-syllable piles?*

7. After the pupils have sorted the words into piles, **say:** *Let's read the words together to check.*

8. Go through each pile of words, reading and clapping each word. If you find one in the wrong pile, **ask:** *How many syllables does this word have? Where should it go?*

Key checks: Do the pupils understand that a syllable is different from a sound? Can they clap for each syllable?

Extension: Encourage the pupils to use a dictionary or book to find a word with as many syllables as possible. This could be arranged as a mini competition with the word to beat being the three-syllable word 'timetable'. **Ask:** *Can you find a word with more syllables?*

Support: Use the pupils' names to practise clapping the number of beats (e.g. Anna (clap clap), Emily (clap clap clap), Li (clap)).

Contraction action

Strand: Reading – word reading

Learning objective: To understand and read words with contractions.

You will need: a whiteboard, whiteboard pens, a text containing contractions (e.g. *We're Going on a Bear Hunt* by Michael Rosen and Helen Oxenbury)

1. **Say:** *We're going to read a story. I especially want you to notice words that have an apostrophe in them.*

2. **Say:** *An apostrophe is a punctuation symbol that hangs above the line between letters.* Ask the pupils to repeat the word 'apostrophe' after you.

3. Read the story, pausing to write the words with contractions on the board.

4. **Say:** *The words on the board are words with contractions. This apostrophe shows that there are some letters missing and two words have been pushed together to make one word.*

5. Point to the first word on the board. **Ask:** *What do you think the missing letters are in this word?*

6. Repeat this process for each word on the board.

7. **Say:** *We're – we are; I'll – I will; you're – you are; I've – I have. The words are nearly the same, but some of the letters are missing.*

Key checks: Do the pupils know what an apostrophe is? Can they say which two words have been pushed together to make the contracted word?

Extension: Encourage the pupils to find examples of contractions in other books.

Support: Show the pupils the two un-contracted words written on the board. **Say:** *The two words get pushed together and some of the letters drop out! To show there are some letters missing, we put this apostrophe instead.*

This is what I think

Strand: Reading – comprehension

Learning objective: To listen to and discuss poems, stories and non-fiction.

You will need: poetry, stories or non-fiction texts about a subject in which the pupils are interested

1. Read a poem or an extract or a chapter from a book. It should be at a level beyond that which the pupils can easily read. Make sure you read with lots of expression. Do not stop to answer questions during your reading.

2. After you have read the poem or extract, ask the pupils the following questions. Make a note of their answers.

Questions for fiction/poetry:

- *Did you enjoy the story/poem?*
- *What was your favourite part?*
- *What was the most interesting part?*
- *Which character did you like the most?*
- *Why did that character act like that?*

Questions for non-fiction text:

- *Did you learn any new words?*
- *Can you explain the main idea to someone else?*
- *Which picture or diagram did you find interesting?*

Key checks: Can the pupils understand the key themes of the text and explain them to you?

Extension: Ask the pupils more complex questions (e.g. 'How did that character feel when this happened?' or 'How do you know?').

Support: Encourage the pupils to give their opinion by offering them a choice (e.g. 'Did you like this part or this part most?').

What about you?

Strand: Reading – comprehension

Learning objective: To think about and link stories or themes within stories to everyday life.

You will need: a range of books linked to the pupils' reading ability

Note: This objective will need to be revisited a number of times during the year. It could be carried out within large or small groups or one-to-one with a pupil.

1. In a small group or one-to-one, look at the front cover of a story book. **Ask:** *What do you think this book is about?* Invite responses (e.g. a farm, the beach, a train station). **Ask:** *Have you ever been there?*

2. In groups of any size, **say:** *I wonder if there are any other similarities between the story and you. Let's read the story and find out.*

3. Read the story aloud to the pupils. Pause regularly and **ask:** *Have you ever done anything like this? Have you ever been anywhere like this? Have you ever seen anything like this?*

4. Following the story, **ask:** *What was the same and what was different about you and the story?* Invite responses (e.g. the characters may visit the seaside, but the pupils may not have visited such a rocky coastline).

Key checks: Can the pupils relate the story to their everyday life? Can the pupils see what is the same and what is different in the story and in their own lives?

Extension: Can the pupils link the moral of the story to real life? For example, if a friendship problem is resolved in the story, can they see how this could relate to a friendship or playground problem in their life?

Support: Support the pupils in giving their opinion by offering them a choice (e.g. 'Do you think the weather could be the same as here?', 'Does the family in the story have the same number of children as your family?', 'Are the children the same age as you?').

You tell the story

Strand: Reading – comprehension

Learning objective: To retell key stories and traditional tales.

You will need: a whiteboard, whiteboard pen, a copy of *Jack and the Beanstalk*

1. **Ask:** *Do you know the story of Jack and the Beanstalk?* It is likely that the pupils will have heard the story or seen a pantomime.

2. **Say:** *Let's read this version of the story. Traditional tales are old stories that have been retold many times over many years. We are going to retell this story later.*

3. Read the story with expression.

4. **Ask:** *What happened at the beginning of the story?* Give the pupils time to discuss this.

5. On the board write 'Jack and his mother were poor.' **Ask:** *Can you think of an action for 'poor'?* (The pupils might suggest showing empty pockets.) Adding actions to the story will support the pupils in memorising specific words or phrases that you want them to use.

6. **Ask:** *What happened next?* On the board write 'Jack took Daisy the cow to market. He met a man and swapped the cow for magic beans.' **Ask:** *Can you think of an action for 'cow', 'man' and 'magic beans'?* (The pupils might suggest hands on their heads for cow ears, taking off a hat for man, waving a wand for magic beans.)

7. Continue prompting the pupils to retell the story, writing notes on the board and adding actions to help the pupils remember.

8. **Ask:** *Can you retell the story from the beginning? How many actions can you remember?* Listen as the pupils retell the story.

Key checks: Can the pupils retell the story of *Jack and the Beanstalk*?

Extension: Write key phrases that the pupils should include in their retelling of the story (e.g. 'he met a wrinkly old man', 'with huge jacket pockets', 'huge beanstalk', 'stretching as high as the clouds', 'thundering giant', 'golden glimmering harp', 'magnificent golden goose').

Support: Allow the pupils to refer to the notes on the board when retelling the story. Draw pictures rather than write words for them to refer to.

Please join in

Strand: Reading – comprehension

Learning objective: To join in with repeating or predictable phrases in a story.

You will need: a story with repeating or predictable phrases (e.g. *Dear Zoo* by Rod Campbell or *Click, Clack, Moo, Cows that Type* by Doreen Cronin and Betsy Lewin), a story with a longer repeated phrase (e.g. *The Gruffalo* by Julia Donaldson and Axel Scheffler)

1. **Ask:** *Have you read this story before? Can you join in with the parts you know?*

2. Start to slowly read the story and emphasise the repeated phrase(s).
   Say: *Join in each time we say that part.*

3. Continue to read the story, prompting the pupils to join in if necessary.

4. **Say:** *Let's look at another story with a repeated phrase.* Repeat the process with this story, encouraging the pupils to join in with repeated phrases.

5. **Ask:** *Did you find it easy to join in with this story?* (This is especially relevant if the pupils have not heard the story before.) *Were the repeated parts of the story helpful to you joining in?*

Key checks: Can the pupils repeat the phrase, with or without prompting? Can they predict when the repeated phrase is due to occur in the story?

Extension: Use a story with a longer repeated phrase (e.g. *The Gruffalo* 'Doesn't he know … There's no such thing as a Gruffalo!').

Support: Show the pupils the text as you are reading so they can see the pattern of the words. Reread the text and encourage the pupils to join in.

Pure poetry

Strand: Reading – comprehension

Learning objective: To learn some poems and recite them by heart.

You will need: a poem (e.g. *Green Eggs and Ham* by Dr Seuss or *Now We Are Six* by A.A. Milne), a harder poem (e.g. *On the Ning Nang Nong* by Spike Milligan)

1. **Ask:** *Do you know any poems?* Allow the pupils time to think, and take feedback.

2. **Say:** *We are going to read two poems. You will then choose your favourite poem and learn it by heart.*

3. **Ask:** *What does learning by heart mean?* Invite responses and then **say:** *It means from memory.*

4. **Say:** *Let's read the first poem through together.* Add pauses at suitable points. Read it through a second time together for improved fluency.

5. **Say:** *To help us remember the poem, we can emphasise the rhyming words and the rhythm of the poem.*

6. **Say:** *Let's learn the poem in chunks.* Say two lines of the poem, and then ask the pupils to repeat them back to you. Listen carefully to ensure the words are correct and that all the pupils are joining in. Continue, two lines at a time.

7. **Ask:** *Who would like to say the poem out loud? How much can you remember?* Encourage volunteers to recite the poem or as much as they can, even if it is only a couple of lines.

8. **Say:** *Well done for remembering so much of the poem* or *Well done for trying hard to say the poem from memory.*

Key checks: Are the pupils using expression when reading the poem (as this demonstrates understanding)?

Extension: Learn a more challenging poem (e.g. *On the Ning Nang Nong* by Spike Milligan).

Support: Learn the poem line by line. Build up to two lines and then four lines.

New words

Strand: Reading – comprehension

Learning objective: To learn new words by linking them to words already known.

You will need: a story book at a level higher than the pupils are able to read independently, whiteboards, whiteboard pens

1. **Say:** *We are going to read a story today that will include some words that you may not know. We will talk about these words and use words we already know to learn what they mean.*

2. Begin to read the story, making it expressive. At suitable points, for example at the end of a page, **ask:** *Were there any words you were not sure about? What can you tell me about this word?* (e.g. funniest) Write the word on the whiteboard. **Ask:** *Do you know what this word means? Tell me about it.* (e.g. It means the thing that makes you laugh the most.) *Do you know other words that are nearly the same?* (e.g. fun and funny). Write these on the whiteboard too. **Ask:** *Is it a short, medium or long word?*

3. Continue reading the story, asking pupils about different words in order to deepen their understanding.

4. You could also **ask:** *Can you think of an action to go with the word? Can you give another example of how the word can be used? Do you know another word that starts with the same letter or letters?* Encourage the pupils to look for similarities between the word you are exploring and words they already know (e.g. beautiful and beauty, grandest, grand, grandparents).

Key checks: Can the pupils explain what they know about a word?

Extension: Ask the pupils to create a word list for the book you are reading by writing the new words and definitions.

Support: Ask the pupils questions about the word. **Ask:** *What sort of word is it?* (e.g. verb, noun) *Where else would we find this word? How many beats/syllables are in this word? Can you draw a picture of the word?*

I know about that!

Strand: Reading – comprehension

Learning objective: To use what pupils already know to understand what has been read.

You will need: sufficient copies of the same book about the topic you wish to discuss (the book should be unfamiliar to the pupils)

1. This session should follow an introductory lesson for the whole class to a new topic (e.g. castles).

2. **Ask:** *Can you remember any special new words we learnt to talk about castles?* (The pupils may remember words such as tower, portcullis, turret, moat, knight, crenellations, battlements.)

3. **Say:** *Let's read the book together and use what we have learnt to help us understand it.*

4. **Ask:** *Did you notice any new words in the book that could be about the topic we're exploring at the moment? What were they?* Write the words on the board and explain the words. **Say**: *So what is that sentence talking about?*

5. **Ask:** *Do you know any stories where people live in castles? Who are the characters and what are their stories?* Give the pupils time to think, and take feedback. Write a list of stories on the board (e.g. *Jack and the Beanstalk, Cinderella, Snow White*).

6. **Say:** *It sounds as if you already know a lot about castles and you have used this to make links to new words about castles.*

Key checks: Are all the pupils joining in? Are pupils applying what they know about a topic to the book (e.g. recalling the meaning of topic-specific words that have been taught)?

Extension: Ask the pupils to explain more difficult words that are likely to be less familiar (e.g. portcullis, crenellations and battlements).

Support: Ask the pupils to explain simpler words that may be more familiar (e.g. knight and tower).

That doesn't sound right!

Strand: Reading – comprehension

Learning objective: To check the text makes sense when read aloud.

You will need: sufficient copies of the same story (e.g. guided group reading books), a puppet

1. Tell the pupils you are going to play a game. The puppet is going to read the book and may make some mistakes. **Say:** *I want you to follow along in your own book. If the puppet makes a mistake, you must say 'That doesn't sound right!'*

2. Misread a word every one or two sentences, focusing on words you know the pupils find particularly tricky (e.g. if the pupils confuse *me* and *my*, focus on these words).

3. The pupils should correct the word and reread the whole sentence.

4. Praise the pupils who stop the puppet and correct the misread word. Ensure that all the pupils reread the sentence correctly.

5. If the puppet makes an error that is unnoticed by anyone, stop and **say:** *Something did not sound quite right to me.* Then ask the puppet to reread the sentence/paragraph with the same error.

6. Finish by asking the pupils to read the whole story aloud, with the puppet listening to each pupil in turn.

Key checks: Can the pupils track the text as it is read? Can the pupils spot errors and also correct them?

Extension: Read a little more quickly and make a variety of mistakes, including decodable and unfamiliar words.

Support: Limit mistaken words to words the pupils will find easy to spot in order to build their confidence.

Why this title?

Strand: Reading – comprehension: discussing the significance of the title and events

Learning objective: To discuss why the author chose the title.

You will need: sufficient copies of a book to discuss (e.g. *Dogger* by Shirley Hughes), other books

1. **Say:** *We are going to think like the author today, and decide why this title was chosen for the book.*

2. Read the story together.

3. **Ask:** *Who are the characters in the story? What is the story about?* Give the pupils time to think, and take feedback.

4. **Ask:** *Do you think the author gave the book a good title? Does it tell you anything about the story? Why do you think the author chose this title?* Invite responses.

5. **Ask:** *Can you think of different titles that could have been used for the story?* (If using *Dogger*, the pupils might suggest 'The Lost Toy'.) *Can you tell me why you think that?*

6. **Say:** *You are sharing your opinion. That is what you think, so there is no right or wrong answer, as long as you can explain why.*

Key checks: Do the pupils think the book title is a good title for that book? Can they explain why or why not?

Extension: Ask the pupils to evaluate or review a book each and to give reasons why they think the title is a good choice or not.

Support: Offer the pupils sentence starters (e.g. 'I think the title fits the book because …' or 'I think the author chose this title because …').

Prove it

Strand: Reading – comprehension

Learning objective: To be able to answer questions about the story, giving reasons for their answers.

You will need: sufficient copies of the same book (e.g. guided group reading books), paper and pencils

Note: It is important to have read the whole text before beginning the session. There is often a teacher's book to accompany guided group reading books and these can be a useful source of questions.

1. **Say:** *Let's think about the book we are reading. We're going to think about the story and give reasons for what we think. Sometimes the ideas in the book may be a bit hidden, but we are fantastic reading detectives, and we will find them!*

2. Read the book together. Then ask the following questions, inviting responses and noting feedback.

3. **Ask:** *How does the character feel? How do you know? What does the character do or say that shows you how they are feeling? What are the words that show this?*

4. **Ask:** *What is the mood of the story at the beginning? How do you know? Where are the words that show the mood?*

5. **Ask:** *What do the characters' actions/choices tell you about them? Are they good characters or nasty ones?*

6. After each question, **ask:** *Can you prove it?*

Key checks: Can the pupils find evidence in the story to support their answers?

Extension: Draw a feelings map for one character at different stages in the story – beginning, middle and end. **Ask:** *How do the character's feelings change? What are the words or phrases that show this in the book?*

Support: Ask the pupils the questions one at a time, and help each pupil to find the page that gives the answer. Explain that the words they need to find are on this page. **Say:** *Be a detective. Look at the page carefully for word clues.*

What happens next?

Strand: Reading – comprehension

Learning objective: To predict what happens next in the story.

You will need: sufficient copies of a book that is carefully matched to the pupils' reading ability and that the pupils have not seen before (e.g. guided reading books), a second such book

1. **Say:** *Part of understanding a story is to make a prediction about what could happen next.*

2. **Ask:** *What does 'make a prediction' mean?* Invite responses and then **say:** *It means to make a sensible guess.*

3. Ask the pupils to look at the front cover of the book. **Ask:** *What could the book be about? Who do you think the characters could be?*

4. **Say:** *Let's start to read the story together.* Read a few pages – the number will depend on the book. Stop the pupils.

5. **Ask** a suitable question, e.g. *What problems do you think the characters may face? Are there any clues that make you think that?*

6. **Say:** *Let's continue to read.* Read roughly halfway. **Ask:** *Were you correct with your predictions? Do you need to change what you think? How do you think the story might end?*

7. **Say:** *Let's continue to read.* Finish reading the book. **Ask:** *Were you correct with your prediction about the end of the story?*

Key checks: Are the pupils able to make predictions based on clues in the book?

Extension: Ask the pupils to draw or write what they think will happen next. They can refer back to their ideas as you move through the book and evaluate if their initial prediction was correct or not. Encourage pupils to see that, if their prediction is different from the outcome of the book, it is because this is what the author made them believe at that point in the story.

Support: Remind the pupils that offering an opinion is what counts; they do not have to be correct. Provide sentence starters to scaffold their answers (e.g. 'I think the characters will have an argument because …' or 'I think the end of the story will be a happy one because …').

Book review

Strand: Reading – comprehension

Learning objectives: To clearly explain what is meant by the text; to listen and take turns in conversation.

You will need: sufficient copies of a book that is carefully matched to the pupils' reading ability (e.g. guided reading books), a more challenging book, a simpler book

1. **Say:** *Today I want you to read a book. When you've finished, I'd like you to tell me what you've read about and if you enjoyed the book. I would like to know if this book would be good for another group.*

2. Read the book together.

3. **Ask:** *Can you tell me what happened in the story using your own words? This is called 'summarising'.*

4. Give the pupils time to think, and take feedback. Ask different pupils each time for feedback, although the whole group should discuss the questions.

5. **Say:** *That's a good point. Can anybody add to what* (name) *said?*

6. **Ask:** *Did you enjoy the story? What was your favourite part?* Again, allow the pupils time to think, and take feedback.

7. **Ask:** *Who else would enjoy this book? Why do you think that?* Give the pupils time to think, and take feedback.

Key checks: Are the pupils able to summarise the text in a few sentences, stating the main points? Are the pupils able to give their opinions about the book?

Extension: Provide a more challenging book.

Support: Provide a simpler text. It is important that the pupils are able to explain themselves, otherwise less confident children may learn to rely on other children or adults to talk for them.

Tap and spell

Strand: Writing – transcription

Learning objective: To spell words containing the 40+ phonemes already taught.

You will need: flashcards (hen, rain, bank, dogs, wait, park, bird, coat, grew, dried, scared, sound, green, garden, threw, church, bright, crawl, chair, August, Tuesday, morning), whiteboards, whiteboard pens

1. **Say:** *Today we are going to use the sounds we know to spell words.*

2. For the words 'hen' and 'rain', do the following:

   - Say each word slowly and ask the pupils to repeat it.
   - Separate the word into individual sounds (phonemes) and tap your finger on the table for each sound (e.g. *hen, h-e-n,* with an accompanying tap for each letter; *rain, r-ai-n,* with three taps).
   - Pupils repeat what you have done, saying the sounds and tapping.
   - Pupils write the sounds and then the whole word.

3. Work through the words below, saying each word and asking the pupils to repeat it. The pupils should separate the word into individual sounds, then write the word. Encourage them to do this by themselves. If the pupils are stuck, support them by separating the words as shown below.

   - b-a-n-k, d-o-g-s
   - w-ai-t, p-ar-k, b-ir-d, c-oa-t, g-r-ew
   - d-r-ie-d, s-c-are-d, s-ou-n-d, g-r-ee-n
   - g-ar-d-e-n, th-r-ew, ch-ur-ch, b-r-igh-t, c-r-aw-l
   - ch-air, Au-g-u-s-t, T-ue-s-d-ay, m-or-n-i-ng

Key checks: Do the pupils know their sounds from memory? Can they spell the words from the sounds?

Extension: Where a sound has more than one letter, tap with the correct number of fingers (e.g. right: r-igh-t, tap one finger, tap three fingers, tap one finger).

Support: Write three-letter words (e.g. man, pip). Avoid common exception words (e.g. was). Pupils practise writing the sound when an adult says it.

It's spelt like that?

Strand: Writing – transcription

Learning objective: To spell the common exception words for Year 1 from English Appendix 1 of the National Curriculum (the, a, do, to, today, of, said, says, are, were, was, is, his, has, I, you, your, they, be, he, me, she, we, no, go, so, by, my, here, there, where, love, come, some, one, once, ask, friend, school, put, push, pull, full, house, our).

You will need: paper cut into strips, pencils, scissors, whiteboards, whiteboard pens

1. **Say:** *Today we are going to learn to spell some tricky words. They are tricky because they are spelt differently to how they sound.*

2. **Say:** *Let's start with the word 'was'. Write this on your paper, saying each letter name as you write. w-a-s. Now use the scissors to cut up the word into letters. Swap it with the person next to you.* **Ask:** *How quickly can you put the word back together?*

3. Repeat with other words. The words can be cut into chunks, rather than individual letters. **Say:** *Cut this word into three pieces.*

4. Play hangman. Write the correct number of dashes on the board. **Say:** *Tell me a letter name. When you think you know my word, write it on your whiteboard.*

Key checks: Can the pupils write sounds in response to hearing them? Are the pupils joining in when asked?

Extension: Ask the pupils to apply their knowledge of tricky words by using them in a sentence.

Support: Focus on shorter tricky words (e.g. to, go, no, he, me, I).

Every day is a good day

Strand: Writing – transcription

Learning objective: To be able to spell the days of the week.

You will need: whiteboards, whiteboard pens, flashcards showing days of the week

1. **Ask:** *What are the days of the week?* Give the pupils time to think and write their responses on their whiteboards.

2. If the pupils have not provided all of the days, add them now. **Say:** *Let's write down the missing days.* Write all the days on the board. **Say:** Remember that all the days start with a capital letter.

3. **Say:** *The days of the week all have the word 'day' hiding in them. What do you notice about where the word 'day' is hiding in the words?* Prompt the pupils to notice that the word appears at the end of each day of the week.

4. Arrange the flashcards in order. **Say:**
   Monday, Tuesday, Wednesday, Thursday, Friday, Saturday, Sunday too.
   One, two, three, four, five, six, seven days.
   Each day different and every day new.

5. **Ask:** *Can you write the days of the week in the correct order starting with Monday?* Give the pupils time to do this and check their order together.

6. **Ask:** *Do you notice anything about some of the spellings?* Allow the pupils time to think, and take feedback. **Say:** *Don't forget that Tuesday starts with a T. Say Wed-nes-day slowly so you remember to write all the sounds.*

7. **Say:** *Let's play a game called before and after. Which day comes after Tuesday? Which day comes before Saturday?* The pupils should write their answers on their whiteboards, remembering to use a capital letter. Ask other similar questions.

Key checks: Can the pupils say and write the days of the week in the correct order? Can they spell the days of the week correctly?

Extension: Ask the pupils to write the days of the week backwards, starting at Wednesday.

Support: Focus on one day at a time. Look at a flashcard, hide it and then ask the pupils to write the day. Use the flashcards to check spelling or for reference whenever needed.

Alphabet antics

Strand: Writing – transcription

Learning objective: To name the letters of the alphabet.

You will need: an alphabet chart, whiteboards, whiteboard pens

1. **Ask:** *Do you know the letter names? We use the letter names in the alphabet song.* Sing the alphabet song together, while pointing to the letters on the alphabet chart.

2. **Ask:** *Why do we need to know the letter names?* Allow time for the pupils to think, and then take feedback. (The pupils might suggest that we say some country names by using the letter names, e.g. UK and USA.)

3. **Ask:** *How can I spell the ay sound?* Give the pupils time to think, and take feedback. Write ay and ai on the board. **Say:** *If you are not sure which sort of ay to choose in a word, we can use letter names to tell the sounds apart.* **Ask:** *Do I need a-i or a-y to spell drain?*

4. **Ask:** *How do I spell cloud? Which ou sound shall I choose?* Give the pupils time to think, and take feedback. Write ou and ow on the board. *Can you tell me which one I should choose using the letter names?*

5. **Ask:** *How do I spell rule? Which u-e sound shall I choose – u-e or oo? Can you tell me which one using the letter names?*

6. Continue with further examples as needed.

Key checks: Do the pupils know the letter names in order and out of order?

Extension: Spell out words using the letter names and ask the pupils to write the words.

Support: Play hangman to familiarise the pupils with using letter names out of order. Write the correct number of dashes on the board. **Say:** *Tell me a letter name.* The pupils must give a letter name to have a turn; if the pupil gives the sound instead, **say:** *You have given me the sound. Can you give me the letter name?* Display the alphabet chart nearby for pupils to refer to.

One or many?

Strand: Writing – transcription

Learning objective: To add –s or –es to regular nouns to make them plural.

You will need: some groups of objects (e.g. toy cars, trains, counters), whiteboards, whiteboard pens

1. Put one object (e.g. a car) on the table. **Ask:** *How many cars are there?* (one car)

2. Now put four cars on the table. **Ask:** *How many cars are there?* (four cars) Point to each car in turn and **say:** *One car, two cars, three cars, four cars.* Write 'car' and 'cars' on the board.

3. **Say:** *A single car, or one car, we call the 'singular'. More than one car, two cars or ten cars, we call the 'plural'. The plural of car is cars.*

4. Put a different single object (e.g. train) on the table. **Ask:** *How many trains are there?* (one train) Now put six trains on the table. **Ask:** *How many trains are there?* (six trains) Write 'train' and 'trains' on the board.

5. Write these words on the board: cow, spoon, house, table. **Ask:** *Can you change these nouns from the singular to the plural?* Give the pupils time to try to write the plurals on their whiteboards. Then check them together. **Say:** *These become cows, spoons, houses, tables. We add the ending –s.*

6. Write these words on the board: wish, fish, witch, brush. **Ask:** *Can you change these nouns from the singular to the plural?* Give the pupils time to try to write the plurals on their whiteboards. Then check them together. **Say:** *These become wishes, fishes, witches, brushes. If the ending –s was added on its own, it would be very difficult to say the word.*

Key checks: Do the pupils know what plural and singular mean? Can they correctly add the endings –s and –es? This builds onto the activity about reading and understanding words with plural endings earlier in the book.

Extension: Ask the pupils to make plural noun forms from a mixture of words requiring –s and –es endings. Can they work out the spelling rule? (Nouns ending in ch, sh, s, x and z need –es adding.)

Support: Ask: *Do you know whether to add –s or –es? Let's try the –s and the –es endings.* The adult should say the word as well as the pupil to support reading.

Doing and undoing

Strand: Writing – transcription

Learning objective: To use the prefix un–.

You will need: whiteboards, whiteboard pens, flashcards (tie, kind, do, wrap, pack, lock, happy), flashcard showing the prefix un–

1. **Say:** *Today we are going to learn how to add the prefix un– (say the letter names) to words.* **Ask:** *Can you tell me what a prefix is?* Give the pupils some thinking time and take feedback. **Say:** *A prefix is a group of letters that is added to the start of a word to change the meaning.*

2. Write the word 'tie' on the board. **Ask:** *If we put the prefix un– on the front of this word, what do we make?* (untie) Make a tying and untying action as you say the words.

3. **Ask:** *How does adding the prefix un– change the meaning of the word?* Invite responses. **Say:** *It changes the meaning of the word to the opposite.*

4. **Ask:** *Can you say what the word will be if we add un– to the start of these words?* Write these words on the board, one at a time: kind, do, wrap, pack, lock, happy.

5. **Ask:** *Can you write the words on your whiteboard and add the prefix un–?*

6. **Ask:** *Can you use the word 'untie' in a sentence?*

Key checks: Do the pupils understand that a prefix is added to the front of a word? Do they understand what a prefix is and what it does?

Extension: Encourage the pupils to write other un– words in the context of a sentence.

Support: Use the flashcard un– together with the flashcards for the root words so that the pupils can see the word segments clearly.

Present and past

Strand: Writing – transcription

Learning objective: To add the suffixes –ing and –ed to create present and past tense verbs.

You will need: whiteboards, whiteboard pens, flashcards (open, ask, walk, help, listen), flashcards showing the suffixes –ing and –ed

1. **Say:** *Today we are going to learn to add suffixes to words.* **Ask:** *Can you tell me what a suffix is?* Allow time for the pupils to think, and take feedback. **Say:** *A suffix is when a letter or group of letters is added to the end of a word.*

2. Write the verb 'play' on the board. Ask the pupils to add the suffix –ing to the verb. **Say:** *play + –ing = playing.*

3. Write these words on the board: open, ask, walk, help, listen. **Ask:** *Can you add the suffix –ing to these verbs? Can you copy these words on to your whiteboard and add –ing?*

4. **Say:** *We can use verbs with an –ing ending (suffix) to talk about actions happening now, in the present. For example, Chloe is listening.*

5. **Ask:** *Can you add the suffix –ed to the same verbs? How do they change?* Ask the pupils to rub out the –ing ending on their whiteboards and replace them with –ed.

6. **Say:** *We call verbs with an –ed suffix past tense verbs. These are actions that have already happened. For example, Callum walked.*

Key checks: Do the pupils understand the words suffix and verb? Can the pupils add the suffix to the end of the word? Do they understand the difference between adding –ing and –ed to make present and past tense verbs?

Extension: Ask the pupils to write sentences using the verbs with suffixes in context.

Support: Use flashcards showing the root words and the suffixes so the pupils are able to build the word. Teach the pupils the past and present tenses in different sessions.

Long, longer, longest

Strand: Writing – transcription

Learning objective: To add the suffixes –er and –est to create comparative adjectives.

You will need: three pencils of different lengths, flashcards (long, thick, weak, smooth, loud, sharp), whiteboards, whiteboard pens, flashcards showing the suffixes –er and –est

1. **Say:** *Today we are going to add letters to the ends of words to make new words that will help us to compare objects.* Remind the pupils what a suffix is.

2. **Say:** *We use the suffixes –er and –est to compare objects. For example, here are three pencils.* Write the word 'long' on the board three times. **Ask:** *Can you add the suffixes –er and –est to two of the words? Now can you place the pencils so they match the words?*

3. Show the flashcards. **Say:** *Choose a different word from the flashcards. Write it three times on your whiteboard. Now add the endings –er and –est to two of the words.* **Ask:** *Can you find examples of objects to match your words? Or draw pictures on your whiteboard?* (The pupils might choose thick, thicker, thickest and draw three different trees.)

4. **Ask:** *Do you think the endings are easy to add?* Give the pupils time to think, and then take feedback. Agree that they are easy to add as they are added directly onto the end of the word.

5. **Ask:** *When do we use these word endings?* Again, give the pupils time to think, and then take feedback. **Say:** *When two objects are being compared, we add –er. For example, this skipping rope is longer than this one. When three or more objects are being compared, we add –est to talk about the last one. This skipping rope is the longest.*

Key checks: Do the pupils understand what the word suffix means? Can the pupils add the suffix to the end of the words? Do they understand how these suffixes are used for comparison?

Extension: Ask the pupils to write sentences using the words in context (e.g. 'This book is thick. That book is thicker.').

Support: Use the flashcards for the root words together with the flashcards for the suffixes so that the pupils are able to build the word.

Write it right

Strand: Writing – transcription

Learning objective: To write a sentence that has been dictated.

You will need: whiteboards, whiteboard pens

1. **Say:** *I am going to say a sentence. Listen carefully.*

2. **Say:** *Anna jumped into the swimming pool.* **Ask:** *Can you repeat the sentence?* Invite the pupils to say the sentence back to you.

3. **Say:** *I am going to say the sentence again. This time I want you to write the sentence exactly. Make sure you use all you know about spelling to choose the right sounds. Remember to start with a capital letter.* **Say:** *Anna jumped into the swimming pool.* Continue to repeat the sentence until the pupils have remembered what to write.

4. Write the sentence on the board and check what the pupils have written on their whiteboards.

5. Dictate further sentences using the same process:

   • The door buzzed and the boy pushed it open.

   • The lady unzipped the longest coat.

   • She had the softest fur of all the cats.

Key checks: Are pupils applying spelling strategies they know (e.g. adding suffixes to words)? Have they remembered to use capital letters and full stops?

Extension: Add further details or extend the sentence by using the joining word 'and' (e.g. 'The door buzzed and the boy pushed it open and all the pupils ran inside.').

Support: Dictate the sentences in shorter chunks.

Perfectly presented word families

Strand: Handwriting – understand which letters belong to which handwriting 'families' and practise these

Learning objective: To form letters correctly.

You will need: whiteboards and pens or paper and pencils/pens, handwriting paper with extra lines

Note: Refer to your school's handwriting scheme of work.

1. Letters are most effectively taught in letter families. Work through each letter family in a different session:

   - Letter family 1: i, l, t, j, u, y
   - Letter family 3: c, o, a, d, g, q, e, f, s
   - Letter family 2: m, n, r, b, p, h, k
   - Letter family 4: v, w, x, z

2. Begin each session with the appropriate introduction. **Say:**

   - *We are going to practise letters from family 1. This family's letters start at the top and go down, then sometimes go off in another direction.*

   - *We are going to practise writing letters from letter family 2. This family's letters start at the top and go down, but then bounce back up and carry on.*

   - *We are going to practise writing letters from letter family 3. This family's letters start in the middle, and curl anticlockwise, before carrying on.*

   - *We are going to practise writing letters from letter family 4. This family's letters are zig-zag letters.*

3. **Say:** *Copy each letter as I write it.* Work through each letter in turn.

4. **Say:** *Practise each letter lots of times. Start each new letter on a new line.*

Key checks: Do the pupils have a comfortable seated position? The book should be angled slightly and the table at a comfortable height. Do the pupils hold their pencil comfortably? Do they need a pencil grip? Can they form the letters using the correct sequence of movement?

Extension: Ask the pupils to write short words using the specified letter so they can practise in context.

Support: Watch the pupils carefully and correct them at the point of writing if mistakes are being made. Build up to short words and ensure they are using the correct formation. Use handwriting paper if necessary.

Neat numbers

Strand: Handwriting – form digits 0–9

Learning objective: To write the numbers 0–9 using the correct formation.

You will need: whiteboards and pens or paper and pencils/pens, squared paper as found in maths exercise books

1. Make sure the pupils are sitting comfortably.

2. **Say:** *Today we are going to practise writing numbers. Our numbers should all be about the same height. They should fit inside one square in our maths books.*

3. Demonstrate each number on the board as you describe it.

    •   **Say:** *Zero is like a larger letter O. It starts at the top, goes anticlockwise round and back to the top. You shouldn't be able to see the join. Now you have a go.*

    •   **Say:** *One is a straight line. Start at the top and go straight down. Now you have a go.*

    •   **Say:** *Two is like a duck's head. Start at the beak and go around its head and down its back. Draw a straight line across the water. Now you have a go.*

    •   **Say:** *Three curls. Start at the top and curl and curl again. Now you have a go.*

    •   **Say:** *Four is all straight lines. Start at the top and take your pencil for a walk down the stairs and along the corridor. Take your pencil off the paper. Draw a new straight line straight down, crossing the corridor. Now you have a go.*

    •   **Say:** *Five has straight lines and a curve. Start at the top, go down the neck and around the tummy. Draw a flat cap on top. Now you have a go.*

    •   **Say:** *Six is like a spiral. Start at the top and curl around, meeting in the middle. Now you have a go.*

    •   **Say:** *Seven is like an elbow. Start at the top, go along the shoulder and down the arm. Now you have a go.*

Continues

- **Say:** *Eight is curly-wurly. Start at the top and draw an S, then keep going to join back to the top. Now you have a go.*

- **Say:** *Nine is a bit like a stick man. Start at the top and draw an O for the head, then draw the straight line for the body. Now you have a go.*

4. **Say:** *All the other numbers are made of these numbers.*

Key checks: Do the pupils have a comfortable seated position? The book should be angled slightly and the table at a comfortable height. Do the pupils hold their pencil comfortably? If not, do they need to use a pencil grip? Can they form the numbers correctly?

Extension: Ask the pupils to write two-digit numbers.

Support: Watch the pupils carefully and correct them at the point of writing if mistakes are being made. Practise fewer numbers in each session.

We're going to the zoo

Strand: Writing – composition

Learning objective: To say a sentence before writing, then write and reread to check.

You will need: whiteboards, whiteboard pens

1. **Ask:** *Have you ever been to the zoo? What animals did you see?* Give the pupils time to talk about this and then take feedback.

2. **Say:** *Today we are going to write about a visit to the zoo.*

3. **Say:** *I went to the zoo and I saw a monkey.* Pause as if thinking and then repeat the sentence. **Ask:** *Could my sentence be improved?* Invite responses, then **say:** *I went to the zoo and I saw a little leaping monkey.*

4. **Ask:** *What did you see when you went to the zoo? Can you write your idea? Start like this: I went to the zoo and I saw a ...* While the pupils are writing, give prompts. **Say:** *Remember to start with a capital letter. What sound do you need next? How do you know you have finished your sentence?*

5. **Say:** *You each need to read your sentence out loud to check it. Make sure you listen carefully; we want to make sure the sentence sounds right.*

6. **Say:** *Next, I had an ice-cream.* **Ask:** *Can you improve that sentence by adding adjectives to describe the ice-cream?* Invite responses, then **say:** *Next, I had a vanilla ice-cream.* **Ask:** *What flavour ice-cream did you have? Write your sentence.*

7. **Say:** *We are going to continue writing sentences about a trip to the zoo.* **Ask:** *What animal did you see next?* (e.g. 'Then I went to see the [big scary] lions.'). [Improvements to the original sentence are shown in square brackets.]

8. **Say:** *We need one more sentence, maybe about something you weren't expecting.* **Ask:** *What did you see that was unexpected?*

Key checks: Are the pupils able to write all the words in a sentence? Are pupils using capital letters to start their sentences and full stops to end? Are pupils making choices about which letters to use to spell? Are they able to draw upon their own experiences to inform their writing?

Extension: The pupils could write a longer story.

Support: Remind the pupils about things they forget (e.g. if they forget to leave spaces between words, remind them to use finger spaces).

Into the woods

Strand: Writing – composition

Learning objective: To say a sentence before writing, then write it and reread it to check.

You will need: whiteboards, whiteboard pens

1. **Ask:** *Have you ever read a story about the woods?* Allow the pupils time to think, and take feedback. (The pupils might suggest *Hansel and Gretel* or *Little Red Riding Hood*.)

2. **Say:** *Let's write a story about the woods.* **Ask:** *Who should our characters be? Shall we have a child like Little Red Riding Hood? Write or draw your own character idea on your whiteboard.*

3. **Say:** *Let's write a sentence to introduce our character. I'll tell you about my character: This is Mary-May and she lives at the edge of the deepest, darkest woods in the land.*

4. **Say:** *Now it's your turn to introduce your character.* The pupils should orally rehearse and then write their sentence.

5. **Say:** *We need a reason for our character to go through the woods. Little Red Riding Hood visits her sick Grandma. I'm going to use the same reason: Mary-May needed to visit her sick Grandma and the quickest way was through the woods.*

6. **Ask:** *Are you going to have the same reason for going through the woods or a different one?* The pupils orally rehearse and then write their sentence.

7. While the pupils are writing, give prompts. **Say:** *Remember to start with a capital letter. What sound do you need next? If there is more than one way to spell a sound, think carefully about which spelling to choose, for example, ee or ea. How do you know you have finished your sentence?*

8. **Say:** *You each need to read your sentence out loud. Make sure you listen carefully everyone; we want to make sure the sentence sounds right.* If a pupil has missed a word, **say:** *Which word do you need to add in?*

9. Continue the writing (e.g. 'She went into the woods and met a clever wolf. The wolf told her to take a shortcut. She got to the house, but the wolf was hiding there').

Key checks: Are the pupils able to write all the words in a sentence? Are pupils using capital letters to start their sentences and full stops to end? Are pupils making choices about which letters to use to spell? Are they able to draw upon their own experiences to inform their writing?

Extension: The pupils could continue to write their own story, including at least four words from a special word list (e.g. crept, sneaked, scurried, wise, clever, creepiest, dastardly).

Support: Ask the pupils to write simpler sentences. Ensure they repeat the sentences out loud.

I like what you've written

Strand: Writing – composition

Learning objective: To talk about what they have written and say what they like and what could be improved.

You will need: a completed piece of writing (e.g. 'We're going to the zoo')

1. **Say:** *I would like you to make sure you can read all the words you have written. Everybody read your writing to yourself.*

2. **Ask:** *Can you choose your best sentence? You are going read it out.* **Say:** *When you read your sentence, I would like you to use a voice a little bit louder than your usual speaking voice, so we can all hear easily. You may need to read more slowly than usual to be really clear.*

3. Invite the first pupil to read out their sentence. If the reader is not reading loudly enough, stop them and **say:** (name) *please turn up* (reader)*'s volume.* The named pupil pretends to turn an imaginary dial on the back of the reader to 'turn up the volume'. The reader then rereads their sentence. If any words are unclear, ask the pupils to reread that section. Make a note of the pupils who struggle to say particular sounds. It may be obvious that a pupil has forgotten to place full stops. **Ask:** *Have you remembered to put a full stop there?*

4. **Ask:** (name), *what did you like about* (reader)*'s sentence? Can you think of two stars?* Invite the named pupil to say two good points about the writing.

5. **Ask:** (reader), *is there anything you need to improve?* If the reader cannot think of anything themselves, ask the other pupils. **Ask:** *Is there anything we wish we could improve about* (reader)'s *writing?*

6. Pupils take turns to read their best sentence and give each other feedback.

Key checks: Can the pupils read their own writing? Can the pupils say what they like about others' writing?

Extension: The pupils could give each other written feedback on a star.

Support: Pupils should be able to read their writing if they have followed the oral rehearsal process to create the sentences, but some may need support. They may need support to say what they like about others' writing. They could start with: 'I liked your choice of words' or 'I liked that your sentence sounded exciting'.

Space it out

Strand: Writing – vocabulary, grammar and punctuation

Learning objective: To leave spaces between words.

You will need: whiteboards, whiteboard pens

1. **Say:** *Today we are going to write some instructions for making a fruit salad. What is the first thing we need to do?* Give the pupils time to discuss this with each other and then take feedback.

2. **Say:** *What great ideas. I will write 'First, you get the fruits you want to use.'* Write this sentence on the board, saying your thought process as you go, but do not include finger spaces between the words. **Say:** *I start with a capital F for first, then you. I know that is y-o-u* (say letter names), *get, the, f-r-oo-t-s (the oo sound in this word is tricky, I know it's -ui-). Then I put you again ...* As you are writing, it is likely that the pupils will stop you to remind you that you have missed out the finger spaces between the words. If they do, continue writing and then go to step 4.

3. **Ask:** *Are you pleased with my writing? What do you like about it?* If the pupils try to tell you about the missed spaces, **say:** *I would like to hear some good news first please!* After receiving a piece of positive feedback, allow the pupils to tell you that you have missed out the spaces between the words.

4. **Ask:** *So why do we need to leave spaces between words?* Give the pupils time to discuss this with each other and then take feedback.

5. **Say:** *Yes, it makes our writing easier to read. Otherwise, I am not sure where one word ends and the next one starts! I would read my sentence as one big long word!* Demonstrate reading like this: *Firstyougetthefruitsyouwanttouse.*

6. **Say:** *Can you rewrite the sentence on your whiteboard and put the spaces between the words?*

Key checks: Can the pupils identify that the spaces between the words are missing? Are they able to put the spaces in the correct places?

Extension: Ask the pupils to write the next sentence in the instructions.

Support: As you reread the sentence *'Firstyougetthefruitsyouwanttouse'*, add forward slashes to show where the spaces should be. *First / you / get / the / fruits / you / want / to / use.* Ask the pupils to rewrite the sentence.

And the next idea

Strand: Writing – vocabulary, grammar and punctuation

Learning objective: To use 'and' to join sentences.

You will need: a picture (e.g. a tree from a wildlife book), prepared sentences on different strips of paper (see step 5), whiteboards, whiteboard pens, pencils

1. **Say:** *We are going to use the joining word 'and' to join two ideas to make a longer sentence.*

2. Display the picture you have selected and say two sentences about it. For example, **say:** *This tree is very tall. Birds nest in its branches.*

3. **Say:** *We can join these two ideas with 'and'.* Write the joined sentence on the board. Ask all the pupils to read it together.

4. **Say:** *Sentences that are joined need to be about the same idea. For example, 'This tree is very tall and we use pencils to write in our books' doesn't make sense because the ideas are different.*

5. Show the pupils the prepared sentences. Ensure they are mixed up on the table. **Ask:** *Can you use 'and' to join the sentences that go together?* The pupils choose two sentences and read them out, joining them with the word 'and'. **Ask:** *Do the sentences go together?*

    *   The rabbits live in a small hutch.
    *   They eat carrots.
    *   The tree was growing quickly.
    *   It had already sprouted new leaves.
    *   The cat drank her milk.
    *   Then she curled up and slept on a rug.

Key checks: Can the pupils match sentences to develop an idea?

Extension: Ask the pupils to add another idea to the sentence using the joining word 'and'.

Support: Spell 'and' together. Read the sentences together. Read out two sentences containing different ideas and ask for feedback on whether they go together.

Stop here

Strand: Writing – vocabulary, grammar and punctuation

Learning objective: To use a capital letter and a full stop.

You will need: a piece of writing without punctuation (e.g. the sample below), whiteboards, whiteboard pens, pencils

---

Foxy looked out of his den he saw Squirrel rush by he needed to hide more nuts winter would be here soon he could feel it

Foxy looked out of his den. He saw Squirrel rush by. He needed to hide more nuts. Winter would be here soon. He could feel it.

---

1. **Ask:** *Why do we need full stops?* **Say:** *It is to allow pauses while we read, so we understand what the writing is saying. Full stops also show us where ideas end.*

2. **Say:** *This piece of writing has no full stops! Can you add the full stops? Let's start by reading the writing.* Read the text together.

3. **Say:** *Now you are going to copy the writing and add the full stops. Remember, after a full stop, the new sentence starts with a capital letter.*

4. **Ask:** *Where does the first full stop go?* Read through the sentences and agree where it goes. **Say:** *A full stop is a small dot that sits on the line. A full stop is so small it makes a little squeak when it's dropped onto the line.* Position the full stop and make a little 'squeak' noise. **Say:** *The next letter is always a capital letter.* Change the lower case letter to a capital.

5. **Say:** *Let's position the next two full stops.*

6. **Say:** *Now let's see if we agree.* Check through the writing together.

Key checks: Have the pupils positioned the full stop at the end of the idea, not at the end of the line? Have they added capital letters?

Extension: Remind the pupils that they have already learned about joining words and **ask:** *Can you join two of the sentences using the joining word 'and'?* (Foxy looked out of his den and he saw Squirrel rush by.)

Support: Read the writing, pausing where the full stops should be. Provide the text without full stops and capital letters so the pupils can add these in rather than copying the whole text.

Ask a simple question?

Strand: Writing – vocabulary, grammar and punctuation

Learning objective: To use a question mark at the end of a sentence.

You will need: a box with an object inside (e.g. a toy animal), pieces of paper, pencils, blu-tack, reading books

1. **Say:** *Today we are going to learn how to ask questions, and write those questions down.*

2. **Say:** *I have a box with a toy animal inside. Your job is to ask me questions to find out what is inside. Your questions need to start with question words.*

3. **Ask:** *What question words do you know?* Give the pupils time to discuss and then take feedback.

4. **Say:** *What, Who, Where, Why, When, How, Do, Does, Are, Can, Is. These are all question words.* Write these as a list on the board, starting each with a capital letter.

5. **Say:** *Who has a question about what is in the box?* Give the pupils time to think and then write one of their questions on the board. (The pupils may ask: 'Can you hold it?', 'How many legs?', 'Does it live in this country?') **Say:** *To show this is a question, we use a question mark instead of a full stop at the end of the sentence. This is how to draw a question mark. Curl around, straight line down and a dot at the bottom.* Demonstrate as you speak.

6. **Say:** *Keep asking me questions. You don't know what is in the box yet.* Ask the pupils to write their questions on paper and stick them on the board. **Say:** *Remember to use a question word and finish with a question mark.*

7. Answer the questions. If the pupils cannot work out what is in the box, provide a 'clue' to help (e.g. 'In the wild, this animal lives in the jungle.').

Key checks: Do the pupils know question words? Can they position the question mark correctly?

Extension: Encourage the pupils to find examples of questions in their reading books.

Support: Provide verbs (e.g. eat, live, play, move). Discuss which question word would be most suitable with each verb (e.g. 'Where does it live?').

A loud, sudden noise!

Strand: Writing – vocabulary, grammar and punctuation

Learning objective: To begin to use an exclamation mark at the end of a sentence.

You will need: a selection of percussion instruments, whiteboards, whiteboard pens

1. **Say:** *Today we are going to learn to finish a sentence with an exclamation mark.* **Ask:** *Does anyone know what an exclamation mark looks like?* Give the pupils time to think, and then take feedback.

2. **Say:** *Sometimes we want to write something and show that it is very exciting, sudden or loud. At the end of the sentence we would use an exclamation mark.* Make a noise with an instrument.

3. **Ask:** *Did anyone jump? What noise did the instrument make?* Give the pupils time to think, then take feedback. Loudly **say:** *The drum went bang! Let's write that sentence.*

4. **Say:** *'The' starts with a capital letter because it is the first word in the sentence. I can sound out drum, d-r-u-m. w-e-n-t spells went and b-a-ng spells bang. It's a loud noise, so I am going to finish the sentence with an exclamation mark.* Make a bang noise as you write the exclamation mark.

5. **Ask:** *Who wants to choose another instrument? What noise does it make?* (e.g. 'The blocks went bang!', 'The drums went crash!', 'The triangle went ting!')

6. **Ask:** *Can we write another sentence about how you reacted?* (e.g. 'The pupils jumped!')

Key checks: Can the pupils position an exclamation mark correctly? Do the pupils understand that sentences with exclamation marks need to be read differently?

Extension: Some exclamation sentences start with 'what' or 'how'. **Ask:** *Can you write an exclamation sentence starting with 'what' or 'how'?* (e.g. 'How noisy those drums are!', 'What a racket!')

Support: Write sentences without punctuation. The pupils copy the sentences and add the correct punctuation.

Who am I?

Strand: Writing – vocabulary, grammar and punctuation

Learning objective: To use a capital letter for the names of people.

You will need: whiteboards, whiteboard pens, alphabet chart with upper and lower case letters, a counter

1. **Say:** *We use capital letters for the names of people. Even if the name is in the middle of a sentence, we use a capital letter for the first letter.*

2. **Ask:** *Can you write the name of everyone in the group on your whiteboard? Remember to start each name with a capital letter.*

3. Changing the names accordingly, **say:** *Write this sentence: Cara and Erik are working with Mrs Blackwood.* Remind the pupils to start the sentence with a capital letter and to end with a full stop.

4. **Ask:** *Can you write any other sentences about the people in our group?* **Say:** *The sentence could be real or made up. For example, The best dancer is Emily. The quickest runner is Kyle.*

Key checks: Can the pupils write capital letters? Do they use a capital for all names?

Extension: Ask the pupils to write longer sentences about pupils in the class. Select the pupil to write about at random by dropping the counter onto the alphabet chart and seeing which letter it lands on. Write about a pupil whose name starts with that letter.

Support: Write a sentence on the board without any capital letters. The pupils copy it and include capital letters.

Fairytale place names

Strand: Writing – vocabulary, grammar and punctuation

Learning objective: To use a capital letter for place names.

You will need: a large piece of paper with a map drawn on it, ideas for fairytale place names (see *The Jolly Postman* by Janet and Allan Ahlberg for ideas), whiteboards, whiteboard pens, alphabet chart with upper and lower case letters

1. **Say:** *We use capital letters for the names of places. Today we are going to make a fairytale map and add some place names.* Show the map.

2. **Ask:** *Can you think of some fairytale places such as 'the castle'?* Give the pupils time to discuss ideas and take feedback. Make a list on the board (e.g. forest, woods, cottage, hut, cave, den, palace).

3. **Say:** *Can you show where the places would be on our fairytale map?* Ask the pupils to draw a place (or simply a dot) on the map.

4. **Say:** *We need to give each place on the map a name. Forest is a place, but it's not the name of a place. The Forbidden Forest could be the name of the forest. The Wolf's Den could be the name of the den. The Perfect Palace could be the name of the palace.* **Ask:** *What other names can you think of?* Add the names to the map, giving them capital letters.

5. **Say:** *Let's write some sentences about the places on our map. Write 'The Forbidden Forest is dark and scary.' We need capital letters for the place name.* Write the sentence together on the board.

6. **Ask:** *Can you write some sentences about the other places on our map?*

7. **Ask:** *Can you write about a journey a fairytale character could make? Which places will they visit?*

Key checks: Do the pupils understand the difference between a place and the name of a place (e.g. a den and The Dusty Den)?

Extension: Link using capital letters for people and for places by writing sentences including both (e.g. 'Mr Wolf lives in The Dusty Den.').

Support: Use more familiar places, such as the name of your school, in sentences (e.g. 'I go to Meadowfield Primary School.'). Pupils can refer to the alphabet chart with upper and lower case letters if required.

Day to day

Strand: Writing – vocabulary, grammar and punctuation

Learning objective: To use capital letters for the days of the week.

You will need: whiteboards, whiteboard pens, *The Hungry Caterpillar* by Eric Carle, alphabet chart with upper and lower case letters

1. **Say:** *We use capital letters to write the days of the week.* **Ask:** *Do you know the days of the week?* Allow the pupils time to think, and then take feedback.

2. **Ask:** *Can you write the days of the week? Remember to start each day with a capital letter.* The pupils write the days of the week on their whiteboards.

3. **Say:** *Let's read the days of the week in the correct order starting with Monday. Monday, Tuesday, Wednesday, Thursday, Friday, Saturday, Sunday.*

4. **Say:** *We are going to write a sentence about each day.* **Ask:** *Can you think about one lesson we have on each day?*

5. **Ask:** *What happens on Monday?* Give the pupils time to discuss this and then take feedback. **Say:** *On Monday we have maths. Monday starts with a capital letter because it is the name of a day, even though it isn't at the start of the sentence.* **Ask:** *Can you write a sentence about what we do on Monday?*

6. **Ask:** *Can you choose another two days to write sentences about? Start with 'On …'*

Key checks: Do the pupils recognise that the days of the week always start with a capital letter, even if they are in the middle of a sentence?

Extension: Demonstrate that the name of the day always starts with a capital letter wherever it falls in the sentence. Ask the pupils to use the sentence structure 'My favourite day is … because …' (e.g. 'My favourite day is Wednesday because we have PE and music.').

Support: Read *The Hungry Caterpillar* by Eric Carle to support learning the days of the week in context. Point out that the days of the week always start with a capital letter. Pupils can refer to the alphabet chart with upper and lower case letters if required.

What did I do?

Strand: Writing – vocabulary, grammar and punctuation

Learning objective: To use a capital letter for the pronoun 'I'.

You will need: whiteboards, whiteboard pens

1. **Say:** *We use a capital letter when we write 'I' on its own, even when it is in the middle of a sentence.*

2. **Say:** *I love reading. 'I' is at the start of the sentence, so it would have a capital letter anyway. Farah and I are best friends. The 'I' is in the middle of the sentence, but it still needs to have a capital letter.*

3. **Ask:** *Can you write a sentence using 'I'? Choose one other person to include in your sentence and an activity to do. For example: Charlie and I like to play football. Mum and I bake after school. My sister and I have to tidy our rooms.*

4. **Say:** *Make sure you use capital letters and put a full stop at the end.*

Key checks: Do pupils use capital letters to start their sentences and for names, as well as for the pronoun 'I'?

Extension: Ask the pupils to extend the sentence by using the joining word 'and' and including other words that start with capital letters (e.g. 'On Monday, Mum and I bake after school and then we eat what we have baked.').

Support: Write a sentence on the board without any capital letters or punctuation. The pupils copy the sentence and add the correct capital letters and punctuation.

Clever words

Strand: Writing – vocabulary, grammar and punctuation

Learning objective: To use grammatical terminology to discuss writing.

You will need: whiteboards, whiteboard pens

Note: Pupils should talk about their writing regularly. Encourage the use of correct grammatical words. In Year 1, the pupils should know and use: letter, capital letter, word, singular, plural, sentence, punctuation, full stop, question mark, exclamation mark.

1. **Ask:** *Can you tell me what punctuation you have used in this sentence?*

2. **Say:** *Show me the capital letters in this sentence.*

3. **Ask:** *Why did you decide to use this punctuation mark?*

4. **Ask:** *Is that singular or plural?*

5. **Ask:** *Does your sentence make sense? Reread it and check.*

Key checks: Are the pupils using grammatical words correctly and confidently?

Extension: Encourage pupils to start using Year 2 grammatical terminology that they have already heard (e.g. noun, adjective and verb).

Support: Provide the pupils with as many opportunities as possible to use the grammatical words listed above. Ensure the adult is not always using the words (e.g. 'Where is the exclamation mark in this sentence?') but instead encourage the pupils to use the vocabulary themselves by asking 'What is this?' while pointing to the punctuation.